Long Island's
Most Haunted Cemeteries

The Paranormal Adventurers
Joseph Flammer & Diane Hill

4880 Lower Valley Road, Atglen, Pennsylvania 19310

Other Schiffer Books by *The Paranormal Adventurers* Joseph Flammer and Diane Hill:

Long Island's Most Haunted: A Ghost Hunter's Guide,
978-0-7643-3293-7, $14.99

Other Schiffer Books on Related Subjects:

Spooky Creepy Long Island,
978-0-7643-2814-5, 12.95

Rochester Haunts: A Ghost Hunting Guide,
978-0-7643-3208-1, $14.99

Ghosts of New York City,
0-7643-1714-8, $12.95

Copyright © 2010 By:
The Paranormal Adventurers Joseph Flammer and Diane Hill
* *Unless otherwise noted, all photos are the property of the authors.*

Library of Congress Control Number: 2010929181

All rights reserved. No part of this work may be reproduced or used in any form or by any means—graphic, electronic, or mechanical, including photocopying or information storage and retrieval systems—without written permission from the publisher.
The scanning, uploading and distribution of this book or any part thereof via the Internet or via any other means without the permission of the publisher is illegal and punishable by law. Please purchase only authorized editions and do not participate in or encourage the electronic piracy of copyrighted materials.
"Schiffer," "Schiffer Publishing Ltd. & Design," and the "Design of pen and inkwell" are registered trademarks of Schiffer Publishing Ltd.

Designed by Stephanie Daugherty
Type set in NewBskvll BT/Gill Sans Std

ISBN: 978-0-7643-3589-1
Printed in China

Schiffer Books are available at special discounts for bulk purchases for sales promotions or premiums. Special editions, including personalized covers, corporate imprints, and excerpts can be created in large quantities for special needs. For more information contact the publisher:

Published by Schiffer Publishing Ltd.
4880 Lower Valley Road
Atglen, PA 19310
Phone: (610) 593-1777; Fax: (610) 593-2002
E-mail: Info@schifferbooks.com

For the largest selection of fine reference books on this and related subjects, please visit our web site at:

www.schifferbooks.com

We are always looking for people to write books on new and related subjects. If you have an idea for a book please contact us at the above address.

This book may be purchased from the publisher. Include $5.00 for shipping. Please try your bookstore first. You may write for a free catalog.

In Europe, Schiffer books are distributed by

Bushwood Books
6 Marksbury Ave.
Kew Gardens
Surrey TW9 4JF England
Phone: 44 (0) 20 8392 8585; Fax: 44 (0) 20 8392 9876
E-mail: info@bushwoodbooks.co.uk
Website: www.bushwoodbooks.co.uk

Chapter Two: St. George's Church and Cemetery 46

Chapter Three: East Hillside Cemetery 54

Chapter Four: Lake Ronkonkoma Cemetery 74

Chapter Five: Union Cemetery 80

Chapter Six: Pine Hollow Cemetery 97

Chapter Seven: Sagtikos Manor 109

Chapter Eight: Mount Olivet & All Faiths Cemeteries 123

Bibliography 144

Acknowledgments

We are blessed to be associated with amazingly dedicated and talented paranormal investigators, colleagues, and friends.

† A special thanks goes to artist Karen Isaksen of Bay Shore, who shared her wonderful talents with us once again.

† We extend our thanks to Mike Salvia, an extraordinary photographer, videographer, and EVP expert, from Old Bethpage.

† Gifted psychics John Altieri, of North Babylon, and Barbara Loiko, of Farmingdale, added dimension and insight to our investigations.

† To Kathy Abrams of Bethpage, we cherish your love and unwavering support.

† Thanks to The Paranormal Investigators, Brigid Goode of Ronkonkoma and Chris Griffith of Lake Ronkonkoma...you guys are dear friends and outstanding ghost hunters.

† To John, Michele, and Tyler Snow of Baldwin — aka Snow Family Paranormal — we are proud to have you as colleagues and friends.

† To Peggy Vetrano of Eastern Suffolk Paranormal...you are a creative and bold investigator. Your photographs and EVPs are legendary among Long Island ghost hunters.

† John and Laura Leita of Long Island Oddities are at the helm of Long Island's paranormal community...your work inspires the rest of us.

We would like to also acknowledge and thank Cyndi Philbin of Kings Park, Angelica Micelli of Farmingville, Lisa Michaels of Islip, John Squires and Jennifer Carroll of Hampton Bays, Kerry Abelow of Amityville, the Wunsch family of Lake Ronkonkoma,

and Mark and Dave Koenigsmann of Massapequa Park for sharing and contributing your stories and photographs.

Thanks to Maggie Land Blanck, who allowed us the privilege of using photos of the *General Slocum* disaster from her private collection, and Daniel Austin, Jr. and Brian Chavanne of All Faiths Cemetery for taking the time to share their stories and experiences. Thanks also to Robert Holden and the Juniper Park Civic Association for sharing rare insights and photographs.

We are grateful to the program directors at the many libraries across Suffolk, Nassau, and Queens counties who continue to provide us with a forum to reach our audiences. We appreciate your confidence and support.

Prelude to a Haunting

A mysterious bolt of light flares from above onto a freshly filled-in grave in Oaklawn Cemetery in Brookhaven. Diane Hill of The Paranormal Adventurers sits on the ground communing with the spirit of the man recently buried there. "I could feel his presence...I know he was with me," she said.

 *Prelude to a Haunting*

A ghostly figure materializes as a mist at Potter's Field Cemetery in Yaphank. The many tiny dots and larger orbs did not appear to any other cameras on this night. The area where this image was caught was the exact spot where a few weeks earlier John Snow of Snow Family Paranormal had photographed a mist rising out of a grave. *Courtesy of Jennifer Carroll of Hampton Bays.*

The Ghost of Grave 580

As of today, Jonathan Henry Haliday, the promising Sag Harbor artist, was no longer a whaling man. He pushed back his thick dark hair with a large hand and stepped off the creaky gangplank of the salty whaling ship, with a thud, onto dry Long Island land for the first time in four months.

The heavy scent of the whale oil carried up Main Street in Sag Harbor calling all folks hither to *The Deserter's* return home. Jonathan knew he was being watched by the curious townspeople gathering on the street and sidewalks to witness the men getting off the great brown ship. So, he swung the canvas duffle bag over his shoulder and smiled broadly at a group of pretty young ladies looking his way.

The ship's belly was neatly packed with fragrant oak kegs filled with whale oil. The weight of the many kegs sank the creaking wooden hull of *The Deserter* into the slapping harbor waters.

People pointed at the hearty men leaving the ship. They marveled among themselves how it was that the leather-necked whalers could spend so many months out at sea hunting the great leviathans without having as much as one home-cooked meal or the tender embraces of their women during all those lonely nights.

Many a humpback's mysterious song had been put to a piercing conclusion thanks to the demand for their precious blubber oil. It was the oil purchased by aristocrats like the very people looking after the whalers as they departed the ship. They bought the oil by the barrel and used it in their homes. It lit their lanterns on dark, cold Long Island winter nights.

Jonathan and his fellow whalers, many of whom were Indians of the proud Shinnecock Nation, hunted the big gray whales in clumsy red whaling boats filled with sharp black iron harpoons. Whaling meant survival through the coming harsh winter months. During the mean season ahead, these men were financially secure to pursue what dreams they wished and do what they wanted with the money they earned whaling during the spring and summer months.

Some of the men were gamblers, for sure; they'd lose their money in no time in the back rooms of saloons in East Hampton or Montauk, or even on dangerous Fire Island where the women had no morals and the men were mostly mooncussers and pirates. Other whalers were pious men — they would tithe a portion of their money to the churches they belonged to in Southampton, Amagansett, and Riverhead. Jonathan, however, was an artist — the only artist aboard *The Deserter* — and he would use his money to buy paints, brushes, and linseed oil so he could tell the stories of his heart on canvas.

During his months aboard *The Deserter* Jonathan had listened intently to the colorful stories the men told of their adventurous travels amid the Caribbean Islands and of other breathtaking experiences filled with danger and fantastic sights. Jonathan, though, had little to say and stayed mostly to himself, sketching scenes of Long Island as the men shared their grand tales of the seas. The pictures Jonathan sketched were scenes he had painted a hundred times in his head and wanted to paint on canvas sometime soon, especially now that he was back on dry land.

Jonathan would always remember with deep admiration the way the Shinnecock Indians thanked the spirits of the whales before they threw the sharp-barbed harpoons into their dark rubbery sides. The red blood spilled like wine into the jealous green seas. He watched the Indians bow their heads to the giant animals before the carcasses were cut up and the blubber was boiled down in large pots over hot red and yellow flames. The liquid that resulted was like gold to the whaling company;

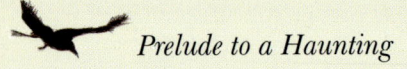

and it was shiny gold that was later paid handsomely to the whalers for their work. The oil was then stored in mighty kegs that were sealed tight with sharp oak pegs to await delivery to stylish Sag Harbor.

Jonathan had plenty of money in his pockets from the pay he received for his work aboard the whaling ship. Many men hereabouts were making a decent living from hunting whales for oil, but with so many ships hunting the mighty mammals it was likely the number of whales would soon dwindle down to next to nothing! This was especially true of the giant blue whales, the greatest mammals alive, stretching one hundred feet long and weighing 120 tons.

Though Jonathan understood the protests of people who said humans should not slaughter the majestic whales for oil, and also the opposite opinion of those who said we must kill the whales because we need their oil for our lamps, he had formed no firm opinion in favor or opposed to the killing of the enormous creatures.

While he held no solid opinion on many issues, the artist did sense the whales were fast being depleted. He had heard the wiser of the men aboard the ship say secretly out of the corners of their mouths that now was the best time for good men to get out of the whaling business because soon the whales would be no more.

As of today, issues related to protecting or exploiting the whales were now for someone else to worry about. Today was the last time Jonathan would ever step off a whaling ship, as he knew he would not be stepping onto a whaler ever again. At twenty-seven years old, he would now begin his life as the artist he was born to be. He was a painter — and this is why today was the most glorious day of Jonathan Henry Haliday's life. Today was the day he became the fulfillment of his God-given potential.

Making a living would be rough, and he knew that, but he also knew he would triumph if he stayed true to his gift. His talent was from God. It was no accident. There are no such things as coincidences. It's all fate!

What's more, Jonathan felt that he didn't have the right to *not* use his gift. His gift was beautiful and truthful. Surely, God would provide for him and he'd survive because his life was all part of a plan that only God understood. Jonathan believed God had a plan for everyone.

What was God? He didn't know. He thought of God as The Universe.

He didn't give an owl's hoot for religion because religion seemed to be more trouble and full of bickering than it was worth, but he did feel God in his heart. He saw God in the pink shades of the morning sky over the waters off Southampton and in the way the beach grass blows in the gentle winds under brooding autumn clouds over the dunes of Hither Hills.

Jonathan wanted to believe that someday God would direct his hand to paint a scene that would inspire its viewers to believe in something greater than themselves. He wanted to believe he would move people the way Michelangelo inspired people with his painting of God just barely touching Adam's finger on the ceiling of the Sistine Chapel.

Maybe his brush strokes would make pictures that would show the true beauty God intended for all of us. Maybe his scenes of Long Island's nature would make people stop and think about the bigger picture and their place in the universe…about what our lives are really all about and the natural beauty of the place where we live.

The young artist celebrated his new life by buying himself a steaming meal of thick beef stew and hot bread with melting butter at the restaurant on the first floor of the American Hotel on Main Street. He preferred to sit outside under the awning

Prelude to a Haunting

in the cold wind of the storm that was coming up, with the rain beginning to pelt the street in hard drops, rather than sit inside with the rich people staring at him. Then, with the warmth of hot coffee and freshly baked apple pie filling his belly, he pulled tight his dark sailor's pea coat, tugged his black wool whaler's cap tight over his long thick chestnut hair, slung his duffle bag over his strong shoulder, and rushed into the brisk November winds and rain to purchase art supplies and begin his new life at once.

He ran up Main Street through the strengthening storm and bought paints and canvases at McGregor's Store. He bought everything he needed to paint the greens, browns, reds, and whites in the scenes of wild Long Island that had for so long skyrocketed across the canvas of his hungry soul.

His paints would shower the canvas with mallard ducks, brown and shiny green, flying low over the golden sere grasses of the dark salt marsh at Mt. Sinai Harbor in late summer — and he would paint majestic ospreys diving straight down at lightning speed for jumping August snapper in the blue creeks at New Suffolk.

On his canvas, he'd brush white rings on the necks of Canadian geese in "V" formations so long and so many that the birds crossed the full range of open blue sky above a golden brown meadow on Shelter Island in September.

He'd paint great blue herons, gray seagulls, white piping plovers, and black crows flying above the aqua waters of the Peconic Bay.

Of the Great South Bay he'd paint the thrashing of a school of silvery blue fish a half mile thick just off the dock in Sayville — and of Huntington and Northport he'd paint chubby humpback calves swimming beside their fat mothers to Cow Harbor for protection from the sharks that lurk in open waters of the Long Island Sound.

Of course he'd also paint whalers in yellow slickers in red whaleboats and gray humpback whales breaching in white splashes above the raging black Atlantic off East Hampton. He'd tell the story with vibrant blue and red paints how the great mammals were harpooned for their blubber and how the Indians prayed thanks and expressed hopes that the whales' spirits were set free.

In the months to come, Jonathan spent all the money he had earned as a whaler on painting supplies and the rental of a cabin in Squiretown, a place located in a hamlet later to be called Hampton Bays. It was an artists' community that was very much in vogue; and in time, Jonathan lost himself in his work so completely that he became at one with his brush… His whole life focus was painting.

He'd roll up his long shirtsleeves and his dark hair would fall into his glinting eyes as he painted — sometimes violently and sometimes softly — like a conductor directing a symphony orchestra. He barely remembered to eat or put logs on the fire for warmth. He worked so furiously he stopped only when he was exhausted and couldn't hold a brush or keep his eyes open any longer.

The neighbors thought he was an eccentric young talent. Since they were artists, too, they smiled at his shadows bouncing around the candle-lit room of his little log cabin and shook their heads, remembering their own days at twenty-seven. They, too, had once been young artists with a passion for painting, a burning in their souls for creation and expression — a burning they would never lose, but which would become tempered with age. They remembered how they, too, worked at all hours of the night and slept at dawn. They remembered the occasional bottle of wine and the poetry. They remembered studying the light falling on the cheeks of beautiful women in the restaurants in Sag Harbor. These same things Jonathan also appreciated.

 *Prelude to a Haunting*

"An artist's life is an exceptional life," he heard someone once say, "because it is raw and fiery and flares this way and that in response to the world. Without artists pointing out what is precious about the world, the rest of us would live flatter, less meaningful lives."

Jonathan was happy. He was doing what he was born to do. How could he go wrong? Why would God not help him survive? Surely, the Creator would help someone He had created to do what He had created him to do, wouldn't He? Why would God give Jonathan a gift and not provide him with blessings?

It was at the rustic little cabin in Squiretown where Jonathan realized one rainy day while staring out past the red shutters and wet hedges that he would never succeed financially in the world like his brothers and sisters because of his gift.

On days like this, when he felt tired and depressed, he stayed away from the town. Sometimes he'd slap on a hat and carry his paintings into Good Ground, later to be called Hampton Bays, where he sold them on Main Street to tourists from Manhattan. However, he quickly found the tasteless tourists passing through town to the resorts out east in the Hamptons didn't really care about Long Island and its seascapes and landscapes as much they did trying to talk him down in price, which was already too low. Not once ever did someone ask him if the scenes he painted were scenes he had seen with his own two eyes.

He soon found he couldn't make enough money to live. He should never have sold his paintings to the philistines from Manhattan whom he allowed to talk him down in price.

Sometimes he thought only he cared about the stories he told in his paintings, including his stories of the disappearing whales of the Atlantic. Certainly, the world would someday be depleted of whales.

As he painted the beautiful beasts, day after day, Jonathan suddenly found that he had formed a very strong opinion about whales, indeed, and that was whales would someday vanish and now was the time to stop their slaughter! With increasing vigor and an urgency in his work, Jonathan painted the animals in all their magnificence so that he could tell the world of the importance of preserving their numbers.

In other paintings, his brush strokes told stories of Long Island nature and pristine beauty that would also dwindle away because of overbuilding, and, he feared, promised to someday be cloudy memories of old Long Island found only in dusty books written by stuffy librarians.

It was at moments like this his gift felt more like a curse because he feared he would starve before ever making a dent in the world. "After all, how can I paint if I don't have a roof over my head and no painting materials to work with?" he asked the heavens when he sat out in the field near his cabin at night and chewed on grass. He'd look up at the bright stars burning in the heavens. "Where are you, God? Why don't you help me succeed as a painter?"

Jonathan decided it was his duty to tell the world not to kill whales any longer — and he would do this in context of Long Island's natural splendor, which was just as fragile as the whale, and like the whale, was subject to man's exploitation and destruction.

Unlike his well-to-do brothers and sisters, Jonathan was a painter...an artist. Painting forms of Long Island's waters was his great love; and besides, if you asked him, he'd tell you he doesn't have a choice in painting what he paints because he is driven to put down on canvas that which he sees. The artists who lived in the Squiretown community understood this passion all too well. They, too, were once like him.

Jonathan would spill his coffee on the potbellied stove down at the General Store on Main Street on Sunday afternoons while standing and gesticulating up to heaven and complaining to the other artists sitting in creaking hard chairs in the circle about all the tired struggles he had to endure just to paint and tell people stories of Long Island on canvas. The artists laughed and patted him on the back, telling him not to give up.

Jonathan scraped by, barely making his rent. He didn't buy good foods because he couldn't afford them. He ate a lot of bread and drank a lot of water. He worked all the harder to try telling his stories of Long Island to Long Islanders because he felt the promise of his life quickly slipping away. Then, over the brutally cold winter Jonathan developed a wretched cough.

When spring came, people realized that they hadn't seen Jonathan selling his paintings in town for weeks. A fellow artist from Squiretown stopped by the cabin to check on him.

Jeremiah Tuthill found Jonathan barely conscious amid bright landscapes of orange and red flowers, golden dunes under the glorious yellow sun, brown and green canvases with scenes of raging dark seas and breathless gulls fighting headlong into the battering winds of a nor'easter. And there were paintings of whales nobly fighting with all their might against the whalers' black, flesh-tearing harpoons.

Jeremiah helped Jonathan out of the cabin and to a wagon. He brought Jonathan to the doctor in town, but the doctor wanted money before he'd do any doctoring.

When Jeremiah Tuthill told the fat doctor that neither he nor Jonathan had any money, the doctor turned away and said he had no time for such "human waste." He sucked on his cigar and shook his head. "Artists!" he murmured with disgust.

Jeremiah then brought Jonathan to the Suffolk County Poor House in Yaphank to get him some free doctoring. He didn't know what else to do. His wife wouldn't allow him to bring home a sick man!

It was a long ride over a bumpy road, and Jonathan was pale and weak. The sleeves of his rolled up shirt and his forearms were stained with the reds, blues, greens, yellows, violets, blacks and whites of his paint pallet. The paints had touched his arms as he brushed madly on the magical canvases, the colors leaping out at him; or maybe he was getting too close to the canvases as he grew weaker and dizzier. He couldn't tell anymore towards the end.

The Poor House was a dark, sinister place of long green oil-painted corridors and harsh faces. The screams of the "insane" — and the sick and dying — haunted the gloomy echoing halls.

The few pale nurses who dragged themselves about were in a perpetual state of anxiety over getting hurt by the "lunatics," especially the stark-raving mad ones on the third floor.

Some of the inmates had their arms and legs strapped down by black leather belts to their white beds because they would hurt the nurses or themselves if they were not restrained. These people shouted curses and evil black hellish things at the nurses and doctors, and the nurses and doctors told them to "shut up, goddamnit!"

The nurses struggled to keep up with the cruddy piss pans and cleaning up the pink vomit of the sick. Most people who entered this godforsaken place as "residents" lived out the rest of their cursed days in this hellhole, but the nurses were not at fault. It was society that shunned these people and threw them away to the Home, and then, when the same people expired, to Potter's Field Cemetery, a short horse-drawn carriage ride away.

Prelude to a Haunting

In Jonathan's absence, his landlord, Howard Cleary, brought a perspective tenant to Jonathan's cabin. The landlord promised the austere, distinguished old man that he'd clean out the cabin of its "junk" if the man wanted to rent it.

The dignified old man in the polished riding boots and a tall black gentleman's hat stepped closer to examine the paintings that the landlord had called "junk" and wanted to know where the paintings had come from.

"Who is the artist?" demanded Professor Harrison. He banged the boot of his cane against the hard wood floor. "I must meet him!"

"Artist?" asked the landlord. "You mean the fool lunatic who used to live here?" He giggled. "Why that fool lunatic got himself sick and was taken straight off to the poor house!"

"He has talent," the professor firmly stated.

The landlord shrugged and scratched his head and giggled again.

Several nights later, a storm as fierce and as wrathful as the voice of God himself on Judgment Day, bore down on gentle Long Island. A sudden blue lightening bolt smashed into a tall dead pine tree that stood next to Jonathan's isolated little cabin. The tree's branches were torn to splinters and the trunk caught fire.

In the wind the fateful fire spread to the humble artist's cabin. The cabin burned to the ground that night, and all of Jonathan's paintings went up in flames. All evidence of his hard work, anguish, suffering, and joy was forgotten by the world in that fiery instant.

Jonathan fell into a deep depression upon learning from Jeremiah that his paintings had been destroyed. Up until then he had been recovering slowly from his illness of pneumonia. It was more by chance than by the help of the staff that he was healing. The doctors and nurses barely tended to any of the many men and women living at this wretched place. There was not enough staff to serve all the residents dinner, let alone provide medical treatment. Beyond that, and as a rule, the nurses, doctors, and administrators were deeply contemptuous of the residents. They referred to them as the *walking dead*.

After he learned that his paintings were gone, Jonathan plunged into a dark abyss of introspection and remorse that's known as the black night of the soul. He knew he had no other place to go and no potential of painting again. In addition to his stories of the whales and of Long Island, his painting supplies were lost forever, too.

After three days of Jonathan not sleeping or eating, murmuring curses to himself, and raising a fist to heaven at midnight, the doctor ordered him to a lengthy stay at the county asylum, also known as the Poor House, the very place he was already a resident. The doctor had forgotten why Jonathan was there in the first place and declared him insane.

The sky was dark that day. The sunlight was short. Jonathan was now a prisoner in hell. He hadn't any money, a place to go, or hope. He was an inmate. The world placed no value on him. In society's eyes, he was better off dead than alive. The people around him hated him. His brothers and sisters cared not about his woes. He would die in this hole. His gift would never find an audience. God had looked the other way. Now twenty-eight years old, he was a resident at the Suffolk County Poor House — and he had not painted for six months.

Jonathan had been mistreated and beaten for complaining. He was called every foul word he had ever heard and then some. One time two of the attendants beat him and hung him by his feet outside a window on the third floor until he stopped shouting obscenities at the nurses, and the thug attendants woke him up at all hours of the night with stupid insulting pranks and obscene acts. The artist in Jonathan, however, was still alive and kicking.

 *Prelude to a Haunting*

Forgotten graves at Potter's Field Cemetery.

Prelude to a Haunting

Reduced to hoarding scraps of paper he came across, Jonathan would sketch on any tiny surface of paper so long as he could find a pencil or a shard of coal. He sometimes drew birds, mostly mockingbirds or mourning doves, on account of their light charcoal color. He sometimes drew the farm animals he could see and smell right outside his room's windows.

"Nobody gives a rat's ass about your goddamn drawings of birds!" one of the attendants shouted at him. "Here at the Suffolk County Poor House, nobody gives a rat's ass about anything!"

Yet, if he had anything worth stealing, that's something to which the thug attendants surely would have paid attention, Jonathan knew.

Jonathan's funeral was a simple ordeal. The family was never contacted about his death so they didn't have any idea he was gone. It was just as well. They were, after all, busy people and knowing of his death would have only complicated their lives.

The wizened driver clucked at the old brown nag pulling the rickety wagon. As they made their way up the dirt road to what would become Jonathan's final resting place, the nag's hooves kicked up dust, stinging the driver's rheumy eyes.

The gravedigger, leaning on a shovel, greeted the old man. "Only one today, Sam?" he said as he looked at the burlap form in the back of the wagon.

"Yup, Digger, just one. Hardly seems worth the trip, but it's too dang hot to hold him till he has company," Sam replied.

Digger grabbed hold of the burlap sack and pulled feet first until the body slipped off the back of the wagon and slapped the ground hard with a thud of Jonathan's head. He dragged Jonathan's corpse to the edge of the freshly dug hole. The horse released a gassy bowl movement as Digger rolled Jonathan with his foot into the grave with another slap and another thud.

Digger looked down at the burlap sack containing Jonathan's body and muttered a silent prayer. He never buried anyone without saying a prayer. The way he saw it was that just because the poor bastard was unlucky in life and ended up in Potter's Field didn't mean he was a bad fellow.

Digger and Sam joked about the food at the Suffolk County Poor House as Digger filled in the grave. "That's what probably killed this poor soul," Digger said with a laugh, and wiped his face of sweat with a red rag.

Jonathan, meanwhile, stood beside the gravedigger, wondering why the man could not see him or hear him yelling.

Digger knocked the dirt off his shovel and, climbing up onto the seat next to Sam, said "Well, that about does it for today."

Jonathan watched the creaky wagon leave the cemetery. He looked down at the mound of dirt at his feet. The waning yellow summer sun was at his back and he was surprised to see that his lonely figure cast *no* shadow upon the grave.

Then darkness swallowed the day — and with night came others like him who stood alone.

1

Potter's Field Yaphank

Location: Yaphank, New York

How to get there: Get on the entrance ramp of the Long Island Expressway eastbound at Exit 67, but do not get on the expressway. Instead, go to the end of the service road and park along the curb. The cemetery is to your right, just past the guardrail, in an open space; trees surround it. You will see the small gravestones once you get out of your vehicle and step over the guardrail.

Description: Small Suffolk County-owned graveyard. Easy to walk, and cars can be parked nearby on the service road of the expressway.

What to expect: Though this place is noisy because of vehicles passing by on the expressway, people have recorded EVPs and taken photographs showing light anomalies and mists. Paranormal investigators have also reported having personal experiences, including being touched, hearing whispering, and seeing moving lights in the surrounding woods.

Mysterious figures come out of the night at Potter's Field.

Potter's Field

One of many paranormal mists surrounding Joseph Flammer and Diane Hill on a haunted night at Potter's Field in Yaphank. Notice how the mist plumes from out of the ground. In fact, a column of the material, once known as "ectoplasm," is rising out of an area of graves.

The Bewitching Hour

Voices are heard in this place — *Long Island's Most Haunted Cemetery* — because the dead are asking not to be forgotten…

Potter's Field in Yaphank is a forgotten and windy place that comes alive at night for ghost hunters intent on making contact with the dead. Almost all the people interred in this forgotten place were at one time residents of the cursed Suffolk County Almshouse, also known as the Suffolk County Poor House.

Located on Yaphank Avenue, the Poor House was five minutes away from Potter's Field by horse-drawn hearse. The inmates were begrudgingly sustained by the charity of county taxpayers. When they died, they were buried using numbers, such as 580 and 732, not their names. No one can tell by looking at the numbers on the gravestones in Potter's Field who was buried in the soil below them.

Diane and I experienced a macabre voice of a ghost at Potter's Field at 2:30 a.m. on an inky September night in 2009. It was the second time we had heard voices in this forlorn graveyard.

Through the accompanying story and photographs, we will relate the unexpected and harrowing experience that followed the ghostly voice on this mysterious night. The reader should be aware that this is a document stating a case for ghosts at the cemetery known as Potter's Field.

Diane and I had been working all night. We first had gone to Lake Ronkonkoma Cemetery — a place we visit often — to document the strangeness that lingers there and then we journeyed to lonely Potter's Field. It was at this cemetery that the ghostly voice of a man came to us just as we were concluding thirty minutes of photography work among the 1,000 anonymous graves in this desolate place. When we heard the voice, we knew we had to stay longer.

Entities appear to visitors at Potter's Field mostly at night when the air grows cooler and it is easier for the spirits to materialize in ectoplasmic form. Voices of the dead are heard because the dead are asking not to be forgotten.

The small gravestones — about twelve inches tall and ten inches wide — have only numbers stamped onto their nondescript gray faces. There are no dates of birth or death. The names of the unfortunate people buried in the soil below the stones are archived in a book in the Office of Suffolk County Records.

No decorations or flowers adorn these graves. The only gift given to the dead at this site is the open sky to which the spirits take flight regularly it seems, particularly during the witching hour of 2 and 3 o'clock in the morning.

This mild early autumn night had been extremely productive for ghost hunting at Potter's Field even before we heard the man's voice. Towering walls of paranormal mists appeared in the flashes of our cameras only to immediately vanish and reappear someplace else in the isolated graveyard.

Are Mists Really Ghosts?

In the days of the Spiritualist Movement, these mists were referred to as "ectoplasm." This smoke-like white mist was believed to be what spirits used in order to materialize into ghosts during séances. Ectoplasm was believed to originate from the medium.

Participants at an old time séance would sit silently around a parlor table holding hands while a medium went into a trance and communed with the dead. While many of these mediums were fakes out to make a buck, there were those who were genuine and many people swore to have seen apparitions composed of ectoplasm during these events.

Potter's Field

A paranormal mist floats above the desolate graves at Potter's Field …

… and follows Diane (not seen) while she is investigating the cemetery.

A mist rises from a grave at Potter's Field. Could this be a ghost manifesting?

With the 1984 movie "Ghost Busters," ectoplasm became a comic prop synonymous with slime. As a result, today's ghost investigators are hesitant to use the term because of this stigma. Instead of ectoplasm, the term "ecto-mist" is occasionally employed.

On this night, sometimes the mists were so thick and so thoroughly engulfing that we grew alarmed at their overbearing presence and how they swarmed curiously around us like pythons in a dark jungle. We felt we were being scrutinized, sniffed, and breathed upon. I must admit, more than once I felt threatened because the mists were entities obviously propelled by a life-energy neither within our control nor within our understanding of reality.

We had seen and photographed paranormal mists many times before. The spirits were with us tonight in this form to interact with us according to their own rules, maybe touch us or possibly even hit us. As bizarre as it sounds, we had experienced spirits *hitting* us before, most notably the spirits at Sweet Hollow Road in Melville.

Sweet Hollow Road is a lonely country road that meanders for over a mile past a graveyard and through a mysterious canyon of county parkland and reclusive residential properties. Here legends abound. What you need to know about it right now is that like Potter's Field, it sometimes reacts to visitors.

Ghosts were all around us during a nighttime haunting on Sweet Hollow Road. It took place right in front of the entrance to West Hills Nature Preserve. I was struck three times on my hand. Indeed, a ghost knocked the camera out of my hand each of the three times it struck me, shouting "No!" the third time it struck my hand. I describe this event in great detail in our first book, *Long Island's Most Haunted: A Ghost Hunter's Guide*.

Our belief that ghosts manifest as mists is well known to people who have seen us speak as *The Paranormal Adventurers* at libraries and other venues across Long Island and New York City. Diane and I often discuss our opinion that even ghosts, despite being mysterious supernatural beings, must conform to rules of nature. We point out that the word *natural* is part of the word *supernatu-*

ral and means heightened nature, not outside nature. How can anything exist outside nature?

Our experiences have told us that as a general rule the temperature must be around sixty degrees or lower for mists to appear. Why spirits need this lower temperature must have something to do with moisture in the air, but exactly how they manipulate water in the air to manifest their energies is a mystery. Of course, paranormal mists do not conform to the standard rule of mists. Typically, a normal mist appears when cold air settles over warmer water or land. Water droplets then rise and hang in the air, creating mist.

In contrast, paranormal mists, such as the mists captured in Potter's Field, appear even when the ground is dry and the night air lacks moisture. These mists are forces — manifestations of entities — not water clouds. Confusing the issue, however, is our belief that water must certainly be a component of the mists.

When I was fifteen-years-old, five friends and I saw a ghost that was white and misty; its body shifted like it was made out of cigarette smoke or a water mist, but it maintained the form of a human. The haunting we experienced on that warm, sunny September day at a creek in Oceanside lasted about an hour. The event is documented in our book, *Long Island's Most Haunted: A Ghost Hunter's Guide*.

Reports of ghosts appearing to people as mists have been handed down through the generations since the beginning of written history. Cartoons often depict ghosts as misty beings that float in the air, defying gravity, like "Casper the Friendly Ghost." The reason ghosts are portrayed this way is because this is how they often appear to people — especially in graveyards.

A paranormal mist appears before the image of Paul Wunsch and his mother at a birthday party. No one in the house smoked and there was no smoke from the candles on the cake at the time. *Courtesy of the Wunsch Family of Lake Ronkonkoma.*

Strangely Appearing Mists

Despite our belief that mists need cool air to manifest, we have, of course, seen mists appear on hot sunny summer days and we have seen photographs taken of paranormal mists inside houses during warm weather. For example, in a photo Carol Wunsch and her family of Lake Ronkonkoma gave us during an appearance at Sachem Public Library in Holbrook in October 2009 we saw thick lines of paranormal mists. The photo shows a mist appearing before Mr. Wunsch and his mother at a birthday party — and they insist there was no cigarette or candle smoke in the air at the time. "We don't know what it is," said Carol Wunsch. The family's curiosity about the nature of the mists inspired them to bring the photo to us.

Mists often will appear to folks in their homes in dry, warm weather. This tells us that the spirits can create mists even when the temperature is well above sixty degrees and the air is dry.

Suzanne, of Bohemia, called us to her home in the summer of 2009 to investigate the strange mists appearing in her home. Sensitive Karen Isaksen and psychic John Altieri came with us. Suzanne said her pet cockatiels often hang upside down and spread their wings when the mists appear, as if threatened by their presence. She believes that the spirit — *or spirits* — in her home are friendly and mean her no harm.

The Mists at Potter's Field

Thus, Diane and I photographed the mists at Potter's Field for about a half hour before deciding to get some hot coffee at a diner and then go home. It was just a few minutes after 2 o'clock in the morning. We are often out until 4 o'clock in the morning on weekend nights, photographing and observing local cemeteries.

As I mentioned, we had investigated Lake Ronkonkoma Cemetery for a few hours earlier that night before traveling to Potter's Field. We were now growing hungry and tired. We were out this late because our experiences with the witching hour had taught us many years earlier that if you want to make contact with the spirits, you should visit them when they are most likely to be active and about — and we have found that hour is between 2 and 3 a.m.

The night was ever so pleasant, however, and we were delighted to be out in the cool air, wearing only sweatshirts to keep perfectly warm. The end of the summer-like days would soon be upon Long Island and we knew there wouldn't be many clear early autumn nights like this left, so we wanted to take advantage of it.

There was no wind at all. Not even a breeze. I had made note of this fact earlier when we were at the Lake Ronkonkoma Cemetery when I told Diane that there was a "zero" mile per hour breeze. In fact, it had been breeze-less all day.

Moreover, not a single cloud could be seen in the night sky. Diane even commented to me how clear the stars appeared when we first arrived at Potter's Field and were standing in the dark beside her SUV. I looked up and pointed out the Seven Sisters constellation. Then I compared the long hazy line of the Milky Way, which was just barely visible in the New York sky, to how brilliantly it appeared to us months earlier, in July, when we were vacationing in northern Vermont and would sit out at night beside a blazing fire and be stunned by the amazing clarity of the stars in the vast galaxy.

So when the mists began appearing to us, we knew they were not the result of water in the air, but were actual spirits. To this day, we have not reconciled the "supernatural" or heightened natural aspect of mists as spirits with the physical necessity of a temperature at or below sixty degrees, but we're working on it.

Peter 2:17 in the New Testament refers to mists as: *These people are wells without water, mists driven along by a storm, men for whom the dense darkness has been reserved.*

Opposite: Mist in Suzanne's apartment in Bohemia... Suzanne says that when the mists come her exotic birds hang upside down, spread their wings, and scream because they feel threatened by the spirit. *Courtesy of Suzanne.*

Potter's Field

A mist appears just after Joe hears a male voice answer "you're welcome" after Diane has thanked the spirits.

Diane extends her hand to the spirit that spoke just seconds earlier.

The Visitation

The eeriness of the dense, dark night is powerful at Potter's Field at 2:30 a.m. As we were leaving Diane looked into the stark void of the thick night and said, "We are leaving now. It was so nice of you to show yourselves to us and our cameras as mists. We appreciate it. Thank you."

"*You're welcome*," a man's voice responded....

"Did you hear that, Diane?"

I heard it as clear as a bell. I had not expected to, of course, and I was startled upon hearing it.

"Hear what?" Diane asked.

"A man's voice said, 'You're welcome!'"

Diane, a Reiki practitioner with sensitive hands, stretched out her left hand. "Please touch my hand?" she asked the spirit.

I took a photograph of a mist looming suddenly before her — *responding to her request* — as Diane squealed, "I feel a hand in mine! IT'S touching my hand!"

At that second, a freezing air — the likes of which neither of us had ever experienced before — descended upon us and chilled us to the bone. It felt as if the mist was passing through us, not merely swarming around us.

Just as soon as the spirit touched Diane's hand, she and Joe were engulfed in a pocket of freezing air.

A mist swirls around Diane… Do you see the alien-like face just above and to the left of her head?

"I can feel the pressure in the center of my palm!" Diane called to me. "It's touching me! It's making contact right in the center of my palm!"

I photographed Diane seconds later when she stuck her hand into the pocket of her sweatshirt because it had grown too cold to continue touching the spirit's hand. We knew we were in the middle of a paranormal experience investigators would call a visitation or a haunting.

At that point Diane moved several yards into the cemetery to get away from the cold air, but the spirit mist followed her. She took her camera from her pocket and snapped off a few photographs. Each of the photos revealed a mist gathered before her, with some of the photos containing forms that looked like legs or arms sticking out of the mists.

Are the Spirits Following?

"We've got to go," I said, still shivering in the *spirit-induced* coldness. "I'm freezing."

"I am, too," said Diane, and then she spoke to the spirits. "We are leaving now. Good night and thank you."

We waited for another response, but none came.

"Do you have anything you want to tell us?" Diane asked the spirits in conclusion.

Potter's Field

We waited to hear something more from the spirits, but nothing came, so Diane said good night one last time, assuring them, "We'll be back soon."

We then turned to make our way out of the cemetery and back to the warmth of the gorgeous night. We were desperate to get away from the freezing mist to the warmth of Diane's truck, where we could bask in the hot air from the blowing heater.

The night air was noticeably warmer the further we got away from the mist. I turned and snapped off a photograph when we got to the guardrail separating the cemetery from the road, only a short distance from where

Top (left - right): 1. A paranormal haze covers Diane as she speaks to the spirits. 2. Diane photographs the mist one last time before rushing to the car to get warm. 3. Diane caught this image as she photographed the ghosts all around her.

Right: This photo was taken at the guardrail separating the cemetery from the road. The mist appears to be *following* Diane and Joe out of the graveyard.

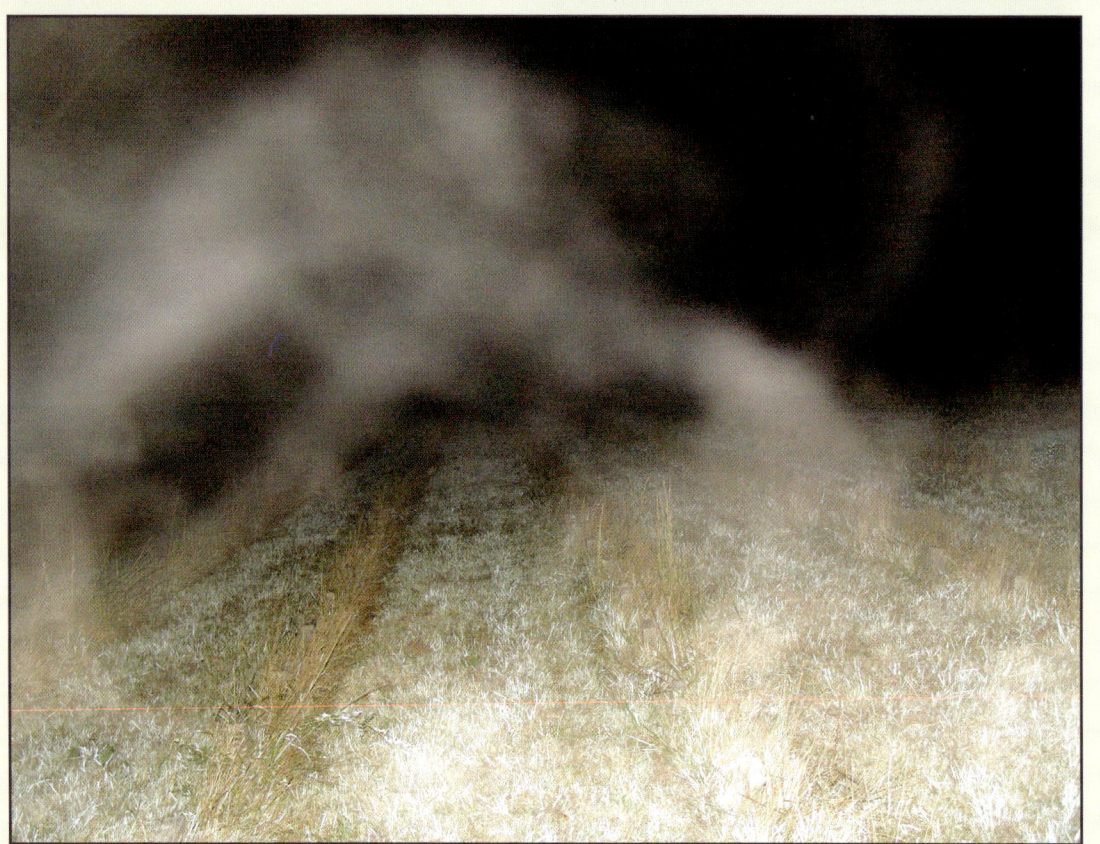

Diane had been touched by the spirit. In the bright camera flash, I immediately saw the mist was following us out of Potter's Field. It looked like a giant octopus morphing its way toward us.

On the other side of the guardrail was Diane's truck — and *an escape*, if we needed it. Diane rushed over the guardrail and opened the truck's door. She sat inside and immediately began speaking to the spirits, asking them for further signs. She had hoped they would materialize as full-bodied apparitions. She did not turn the car on. Instead, she gazed out her windshield at the night, her camera in hand, poised to take a photograph at the first hint of an apparition.

I knew the mist was coming after us, so I stood outside the truck and documented its changing shape as it approached.

Conclusion

The frigid air made it impossible to want to photograph any longer. I abandoned the photography outside the truck and rushed to the passenger door and got in the vehicle. I told Diane to turn the truck on and get us out of there as quickly as possible — before the mist could get inside the truck and maybe change its shape into a decomposing dead person or a howling apparition.

Diane turned the key, shifted to "Drive," and shot her black Element onto the Long Island Expressway's entrance, located only a few yards away from where we were parked. As we drove off, I looked around the backseat, hoping I would not see a grotesque corpse-like ghost. I photographed the backseat and immediately studied the camera's LCD screen. There was nothing there. I was glad.

I knew the mist's appearance outside the SUV was a sign of the spirit's *intelligent* interaction with us, so I asked the spirits of Potter's Field to stay at the cemetery and not attach themselves to us — just in case there was a spirit in the backseat that I couldn't see.

We decided to bypass the hot coffee and get right to our studio to review the photos from Potter's Field. When we got home, I told Diane that it was a man's voice that I had heard and it had sounded nearby, but as if trapped under a blanket. I later wrote in my journal:

> "It sounded as if the voice was speaking from behind a thick veil that separated dimensions between the living and the dead. The voice was not shouted, not spoken loudly. Rather it was spoken at a normal volume. It was a mature man's voice. I believe it was an elderly man's voice."

Diane and I talked until dawn as we studied the photos. We discussed the nature of mists and why spirits remain with their bodies in graveyards after death, but try as we did, we could not come to terms with how or why *they* would want to stay with their decomposed bodies in the graves.

This issue would be the center of our conversations for most of the next day as we walked the streets of Greenport during the village's "Pirate Harvest Festival" in which some people were dressed up as ghosts in anticipation of Halloween, but their Hollywood costumes only seemed ridiculous to Diane and me.

"They should only know," Diane said.

"But is first-hand knowledge of ghosts really knowledge people should possess?" I asked her.

 *Potter's Field*

In these four photos, you see the sequence in which the spirit mist followed the authors out of the cemetery. It shape-shifted as it approached the vehicle, surrounding the truck and Joe. It seemed to look inside the truck at Diane and then went around to the opposite side of the vehicle, pursuing Joe as he tried to escape its biting cold air.

Notice the mist coming over the bushes in the top right side corner of the first photo. The ghost mist of Potter's Field followed Diane and Joe out of the graveyard to Diane's SUV. Diane was inside the vehicle talking to the spirit, asking for a last sign of its presence, while Joe photographed the mist overtaking the SUV.

The ghostly mist engulfed Joe and followed him as he moved away from the vehicle. The mist then engulfed the SUV. Joe thanked the spirit before getting into the SUV to escape the oppressive cold air that the mist brought. He then searched the backseat to make sure a spirit had not entered the vehicle.

Another Disembodied Voice

We received a telephone call from our good friend Brigid Goode of The Paranormal Investigators a week after Diane and I had experienced the disembodied voice at Potter's Field saying, "You're welcome."

Goode, a Ronkonkoma resident, said she and other friends of ours, John and Michele Snow of Snow Family Paranormal from Baldwin, were going to visit Potter's Field that upcoming Saturday night and wanted to know if we'd like to join them on a nighttime investigation.

We had investigated with Goode and the Snows several times prior and admired their work. During one of those investigations — when Michele Snow and I were in the basement of a reputedly haunted house in Holbrook — we heard three extremely loud bangs on the wall immediately beside us in response to the question: "Can you please give us a sign you are here with us?" We jumped at the banging and confirmed by walkie-talkie with the other participating investigators that no one was even near the wall of the house when the banging occurred.

On the night of the investigation, we arrived late at Potter's Field, around 11 p.m. Brigid and the Snows were standing in a circle beside their vehicle near the guardrail separating the cemetery from the road. The Snows' seventeen-year-old son, Tyler, a bright and energetic young man, was joining us on this night.

The hood of Brigid's sweatshirt was up over her head because a light rain was falling. Drizzle had been coming down for about twenty minutes now and the investigators explained they were just leaving the cemetery because of the rain. However, they had a few unusual experiences they wanted us to know about. I grabbed our voice recorder from my car and documented their stories:

"We were in the graveyard and I took a look behind me — about fifteen feet away from me I saw a shadow passing," reported John. "It could have been shadows caused by lights on the LIE, but I had the feeling it was something far more unusual."

While at the back of the cemetery, both John and his son, Tyler, heard what they said sounded like a woman's voice. Tyler thought he heard the woman say his name, "Tyler."

"I heard a female voice, and I thought it was my mother, but my mother said something right after it," Tyler said. "The woman's voice I heard sounded like it was further away. My mother was closer than where I heard the voice coming from."

Brigid said she heard the voice, too. She described the woman's voice as "an undertone underneath the voices of John and Tyler," who were talking at the time that she heard it. "It was underneath, so you couldn't really tell what it was saying, but you knew it was a female voice." At that point, Brigid switched on her voice recorder to capture the voice, "but my recorder would not turn back on," she said.

Finally, as the group was preparing to leave, John snapped off a last photograph and caught a mist appearing out of a grave. It would be the only mist captured that night on film.

As Diane and I drove off into the night, we wondered what Brigid and the Snows would have experienced in the cemetery that night had it not begun raining. We could only assume they were at the threshold of a full-blown haunting as we had been when the mists were shape-shifting around us.

Potter's Field

Brigid Goode of The Paranormal Investigators joins John, Michele, and Tyler Snow of Snow Family Paranormal on a haunting night at Potter's Field.

Mist rising out of a grave. This photo was taken after an hour of investigating, just after the investigators decided they were going to leave Potter's Field. Earlier, a few of the investigators had heard what they believed was the mumbling of a woman's voice. One investigator experienced equipment failure. *Courtesy of John Snow of Snow Family Paranormal.*

More Ghostly Activity

On a pleasant night a few weeks later a chance meeting at Potter's Field with ghost hunting enthusiasts John Squires, Jennifer Carroll, and their friend Stefan would reveal a second sighting of ghostly activity at the same general place in the graveyard where John Snow had snapped a white ecto-mist emerging from a grave.

On this night Diane and I were being filmed by a crew from Phoenix, Arizona, that had attended our lecture at Queens Central Library in Jamaica that afternoon. We had been doing interviews with the crew inside the darkened graveyard when a car pulled up to the guardrail, and out emerged the three young curiosity seekers. We initially thought they were police and a conversation ensued. They explained they were not really ghost hunters, but were interested in finding out more about Potter's Field.

Ironically, only a week earlier, John and Jennifer had attended a lecture Diane and I gave at the Hampton Bays Public Library. Stirred by our discussion, photos, and video of Potter's Field, the couple now wanted to see for themselves what it was like in the cemetery at night.

I took a break from the rest of my group after we concluded filming and walked to the opposite end of the cemetery to engage the three visitors from Hampton Bays in a discussion about the paranormal. I knew if there was anybody who might have a point of view about the history of this graveyard and the paranormal it would probably be John Squires; he is a brazen writer with a lively weblog, "Freddy in Space" (www.freddyinspace.com), in which Diane and I were victims of entertaining light sarcasm after John saw us speak at the local library in 2008. Moreover, I knew John was a descendent of an impressive Long Island bloodline, the Squires of Hampton Bays, of which Diane and I had knowledge through our research of historic Long Island events.

Historians say Ellis Squires founded the hamlet of Good Ground, the earlier name for Hampton Bays, after single-handedly sailing and rowing a clumsy whaleboat from Maine to Southampton with his wife and their nine children aboard. Then he maneuvered the boat to an interior area of Long Island known as Red Creek. The Squires were the first white family to settle the place known today as Hampton Bays.

Additionally, John Squires is related to Captain William H. Squires, who bravely died after the *Louis V. Place* schooner shipwrecked off Fire Island in a horrific snow storm in February 1895. It's said that the captain's frozen body fell overboard into the icy sea and drifted thirty miles east against the current to his hometown of Good Ground so he could be buried with the rest of his family in Good Ground Cemetery. One legend says the captain's body was found only yards away from his home.

The Long Island Maritime Museum in West Sayville exhibits a photo of the *Louis V. Place* shipwreck on a prominent wall. On a nearby written display it raises the question as to whether or not an image people said they had seen in the rigging of the doomed ship was the ghost of Captain Squires, for the likeness was uncanny, some said. A photograph from the time captured the image of the face — and it is this photograph that is displayed on the museum's wall. Diane and I published an article about this mysterious event in *Dan's Papers*, a magazine in the Hamptons, in 2008.

While we talked, Jennifer Carroll casually photographed the graveyard, stopping from time to time in the dark to discuss her personal beliefs and experiences, or to raise a point. As she photographed the graves, it became increasingly apparent to me, like a kettle that was starting to whistle, that the mists of the cemetery were becoming evermore awakened and Jennifer was nonchalantly capturing their forms in her photographs. No one from my group had gotten any mists that night, despite our expensive infrared technology and other impressive recording equipment — but Jennifer was getting them!

Jennifer captured one photograph in particular, exhibited at the beginning of "A Prelude to A Haunting" at the start of this book, of what surely looks like a ghostly body emerging out of the ground and walking across the graveyard towards her. This photograph was shot in the same spot where John Snow caught a mist also rising out of a grave.

As this was taking place, I dared not tell John Squires what I knew and that he didn't know at the time — a man who might have been a relative, James Squires, was buried in that part of Potter's Field where he was standing. James Squires died at age sixty-four in 1893. His grave marker is 732 — the area where Jennifer caught the image of the man. The question that arises for me is: Were all the coincidences that brought John Squires to the graveyard that night intended to lead him to James Squires' grave?

Potter's Field

Potter's Field in Yaphank is the end of the road for some of Suffolk's abysmally poor, developmentally disabled, and frail. There are no names or dates on the simple stones marking their final resting place. Could this be the reason the spirits are so restless?

The Long Island Expressway's entrance ramp is on the left.   End of the entrance ramp.   Grave markers for the forgotten dead at Potter's Field.

Potter's Field: End to a Journey

Cemetery for the "Insane"

Up until the 1950s "Potter's Field" in Yaphank was the end of the road for people so poor or frail the taxpayers of Suffolk County had to provide for them even in death.

The people interred in this forgotten place known as "Potter's Field" — a Biblical name for the place Judas was buried after he hanged himself for betraying Jesus for thirty pieces of silver — were at one time residents of the Suffolk County Almshouse established in 1870. The Almshouse was also known as the Suffolk County Asylum, the Suffolk County Poor House, and the Suffolk County Home for the Insane before finally just being called the "Suffolk County Home."

In reality, many of the men and women who lived at the Poor House were sixty-years-old or older; these people might have suffered from Alzheimer's disease or dementia, or were frail and had no place to live and no one to take care of them, and no means to hire help. In short, they could have been us.

Potter's Field was only a short five-minute ride by horse-drawn wagon from the Suffolk County Almshouse. A casket made of unpainted rough-hewn pine boards lay in the back of a creaky wagon pulled tiredly by an old black horse to the graveyard. In later years, when Ford trucks were available, this task would be accomplished with an old dented-up red farm truck belonging to the county farm.

It's unclear whether all the men and women buried in Potter's Field were buried in caskets, but what is clear is that

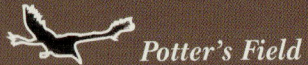
Potter's Field

Artist's rendering of the Suffolk County Almshouse from Suffolk County Historical Records.

Potter's Field

Top Left: Demands were many at the Suffolk County Almshouse. The residents had to be up at dawn and in bed at dusk. They had to eat according to inflexible schedules and follow unforgiving rules. Center: Pictured is the newer Suffolk County Home that replaced an older more inefficient building. Top Right: The Suffolk County Farm is located directly behind the Home.

they were put in a hole in the ground, covered up, and most were happily forgotten about by the world forever. The rows of tiny grave markers are so unimposing and insignificant on the landscape of the graveyard that they hardly draw the attention of anyone looking directly at them.

Life at the Asylum

Besides the abysmally poor and frail, the Asylum took in people who were homeless and in great need or shunned by society, such as individuals with developmental disabilities and mental illnesses. Records available at the county's archives office in Riverhead also show that "pauper Indians," chiefly from the Shinnecock tribe, also took residence at the Almshouse.

Those people who suffered from mental illnesses, such as schizophrenia or depression, or developmental disabilities such as mental retardation or autism, or were brain injured, went undiagnosed and untreated for their conditions.

Those who were able to had to work on the county farm or elsewhere, as there were strict rules of living that had to be followed. People were classified by their level of insanity and segregated accordingly. Men were located in a different area of the building than women.

Residents of this godforsaken place could smell the potent stench of manure stinking up the farm they worked during the day because it was situated right outside their windows. They worked right alongside inmates from the Suffolk County Jail, also located nearby. Both groups ate the eggs of hens on the farm and the meat of pigs they slaughtered. They also ate the fruits and vegetables they grew on the land.

Certainly, life was a depressing experience in the Poor House. It was not a place anybody wanted to be. It was the end of the road.

Potter's Field

On all sides of the cemetery are trees, but on only three sides are the deep woods owned by the county. Nearby, to the south, is the county's Public Works property where piles of sand and dirt are stored.

An End to a Journey's End

With only a handful of exceptions, when the people from the asylum died, they were buried in graves at Potter's Field.

Almost all of these graves were marked with small cement makers with numbers. Records indicate that some of the people buried in this fashion were later removed from the cemetery and re-buried by their families in other places. Many families must have been remorseful that they couldn't have taken better care of the family member who died at the Poor House.

In the early 1900s, a play was written about the poorhouses that existed throughout the country. It was called "An End to a Journey's End."

Today, Potter's Field is still the end of a journey's end. It's the end of the road, but in this case, the end of the road is the ramp used by travelers to enter onto the eastbound side of the Long Island Expressway at Exit 67. The service road ends right at the point where the open space of the cemetery begins.

Parking for Potter's Field is at the end of the entrance ramp where vehicles can go no further without getting onto the Expressway. Cars and trucks speed by to the left side of this spot as they enter onto the eastbound Long Island Expressway and vanish into the insanely active world of the living.

Atrocities at the Poor House

> Lucky Downs charges that, while the girls and the two men were together at the Galt House, in Chicago, Williams was criminally intimate with her, and Louden with Maggie O'Neill, and states that the intimacy of the keepers with the female inmates is common talk in the Almshouse in Yaphank.

According to articles that appeared in the *New York Times* beginning September 12, 1878, at least two officials from the Almshouse — Superintendent Stephen Williams and Keeper John Louden — were accused of immorality with pauper girls who were inmates of the home.

The accusations alleged that the men had taken girls from the Almshouse on a trip to Chicago under assumed names, supposedly to get the girls jobs in a place where nobody knew of their blemished pasts as inmates at the Almshouse. One of the two girls who made the accusation gave birth to a child a year after she became a resident of the Almshouse.

An investigation into the Chicago trip was launched, but after a second story about the problems, the *New York Times* does not report anymore on the investigation of the accusations.

In the newspaper's last report, the men had turned the accusations of one girl who said the superintendent was intimate with her into a pack of pithy lies, taking the spotlight off themselves and redirecting it at the immoral character of the girl. At that point, it seemed the accusations would just fade away into forgotten echoes — and apparently they did.

Gravestone 580

It was a sunny afternoon in late spring when we arrived at Potter's Field for another investigation. We had been there many times before, but today Diane and I were compelled to visit because of a dream I had the night before. In the dream, a young man of low means and in a shabby long dark jacket stood over a grave and pointed at its marker. The number of the grave was 580.

Gathering our equipment, we climbed over the guardrail at the end of the service road and onto a sort of dirt road of rutted tire tracks in the grass. If you didn't know better,

 *Potter's Field*

Potter's Field

...were just looking at a meadow. The tall weeds ...ted the 1,000 cement grave markers. Markers ...ounded tops while markers 501 to 1,000 have ...wo groups of grave markers are separated by ...ugh for a truck to drive through.

...ene doesn't tell the whole story. The souls ly-...anonymous graves had suffered humiliations ...mental pain. They were the despairing. They ...lived hard lives up to the end, fraught with ...mental illness, abuse, shame, and a lack of ...one, especially those who took care of them. ...had their dreams stolen from them.

...ed by Suffolk County tell a shocking story ...nd anonymous deaths. In one case, a man ...a nearby train station and was buried at ...ody knew who he was or who loved him. ...a man was found dead near the "manor." ...s life.

...were buried alongside stillborns and ...d in the Suffolk County Children Home, ...erty near the Asylum and the farm. It's ...uman being's life could be so insignifi-...k County Poor House it seems the lives ...eld no value.

...Clerk's Historical Documents Library ...ed to the Almshouse's history reports

...Works Administration publication, The ...e Poor House became a catch-all for all ...Criminals, lunatics, cripples — all were ...of with the poverty-stricken. The Poor House was the solution to a wide range of social ills. No consideration was given to either the person who was called an "inmate," or to the cause of his or her problem. The records in the collection, as well as the numbered headstones in the cemetery in Yaphank, are a reflection of the historical social attitudes. In 1929 New York State mandated that all institutions known as a "poor house" or an "almshouse" change the name. As a result, the Suffolk County Almshouse changed its name to the Suffolk County Home." *(www.wotan.liu.edu/~mptakacs/almshouserecords.html)*

A lingering sadness hung in the air as Diane and I walked carefully among the forgotten graves, searching for grave 580. The tall weeds made the search all the more difficult, but eventually we stood before the marker we sought. I pointed down at the grave, realizing, suddenly, I was pointing at stone 580 the same way the man in my dream had pointed.

Lying across the grass and weeds at the base of the marker was a long brown feather. It was probably from one of the red tail hawks that we often see flying overhead whenever we visit this cemetery. It reminded me of an old time quill pen. Perhaps at one time just such a quill was used by an artist to sketch this sunny meadow.

"580," I said aloud, just as an unseen hawk screamed from the woods.

The dream, the grave, the hawk — what did all of this mean?

I walked into the woods while Diane stayed behind in the cemetery. These are lonely woods of dim light and quiet solitude even in the daytime. The drone of vehicles whizzing by on the Long Island Expressway fades away into the background. Only the occasional screams of birds shatter the peace.

Ready to Write a Book?

Are you fascinated by the paranormal? Do you turn the conversation at every dinner party toward the otherwordly? Are you ready to share all the stories you've heard, and to investigate further?

We're eagerly seeking authors to pen local ghost story books. If this idea appeals to you, we'd love to hear more. Email your book idea to: info@schifferbooks.com or write to Acquisitions, Schiffer Publishing, Ltd. 4880 Lower Valley Rd., Atglen, PA 19310, or call 610-593-1777 to make an appointment to speak with an editor.

Potter's Field

In the woods, I saw mounds of dirt had formed above the roots of trees. Sometimes there was no obvious reason for other mounds. There is always the concern that the mysterious mounds are covering dead bodies. After all, these are the Long Island Pine Barrens — dead people are found from time to time in these woods, typically decapitated so dental records and photographs can't identify them and with their hands removed so they can't be identified by fingerprints. The police theorize these are mob-related executions.

The vast majority of such bodies are found in the nearby Manorville Pine Barrens, the densest of pine trees on Long Island. The trees are important to Long Island because their roots bind up sand in such a way that the sand protects the groundwater by filtering rainwater. Vast areas of the trees are protected. Ironically, the pine barrens serve killers by providing open space to dump their victims.

Behind scraggly bushes, I spot a pair of green shorts embedded in one of these mounds and resist the urge to pick them up with a stick and inspect them for bloodstains. After all, I am not here to find dead bodies — I am here to find ghosts.

As I walk, I talk to the spirits: "We are ghost hunters," I begin.

I speak to the trees and the spaces between them. "We came here today to try to learn about the nature of your existence. We don't know what happens to us after our worldly lives and deaths."

I wait.

"Can you show me a sign that you are here and hearing me?"

I wait some more, but there would be no sign.

This is an all too common a response — *or lack of response* — from the spirits at such supposedly haunted places. In all but a few of the many dozens of reputedly haunted homes that Diane and I investigated over the years did anything obviously paranormal ever occur. Today, at Potter's Field, it would be no different.

In one case — the Daniel Akner House in Freeport, in front of a *Newsday* photographer and a *Newsday.Com* videographer — a butler's bell went off at the rear of the beautiful old Victorian, seemingly by itself! The ghostly event was thrilling because Daniel had forewarned us that the ringing bell occurs from time-to-time.

In another case, something was thrown at me from across the room while I was sitting at a table with other paranormal investigators in a famous north shore Gold Coast mansion at midnight. What sounded like a small stone flew past my head, hit a wall, and bounced along the floor.

"What was that?" asked Brigid Goode of The Paranormal Investigators. She looked around the room and asked, "Who are you?"

I jumped up from the table and searched for the stone with a flashlight, but found neither what was thrown nor what threw it.

Matt Haas, of Light Paranormal Research, had invited us to the mansion for the investigation and he said that strange events often happened in the house. I later reviewed video of light anomalies he had captured flying through the rooms.

In only a few cases, such as the case of Kathy Abrams House in Bethpage, did Diane and I ever see a shadow or a ghost with a shape resembling a human's. In this case, the ghost was a blue haze that moved about the room. We took turns watching it through the screen of our video camera because it could only be seen with the aid of the camera's Nightshot infrared feature. The ghost threw a pencil across the room and knocked other things around. It turned on a computer right in front of us and breathed in our ears.

Most of the day-to-day investigations that Diane and I participate in come up empty for evidence, with just a few hints of spiritual activity. In this way, our results often parallel the results of many other ghost hunters, including Jason, Grant, and Steve of the television show "Ghost Hunters" and what they experience when they conduct TAPS investigations. Often they pick up on the energies of spirits in a place rather than actually seeing the spirit or a ghost.

We joined Jason, Grant, and Steve on a three-day investigation of the Houghton Mansion in North Adams, Massachusetts, in the spring of 2007. This is a place with a tragic and sad love story behind it. A string of deaths are connected to the house. We were there with other Long Island investigators and ghost hunters from all around the country.

At one point I was fortunate enough to find myself standing together with Jason in the dark at the foot of a staircase on the second floor of the old haunted mansion. He had his Minolta digital camera set up on a tripod and was taking shots from time to time. It was midnight. This was my opportunity to ask the master ghost hunter questions. He has loads of experiences with ghosts, so I asked the questions that I've long wanted to ask him and we compared notes.

My leading question was about the strange faces and forms that seem to appear on trees and in bushes in a given environment, say, for example, in the woods around Potter's Field. I asked him if he thinks the appearance of these faces in photos is all "matrixing" or does he think there's a supernatural aspect to the appearance of these strange forms and faces.

He told me he often gets "cartoonish" looking faces in his photos at haunted sites. The faces appear neither human nor animal, but hybrids of humans — like cartoon faces — and it is exactly these cartoon-like appearances that often occur in our photographs at Potter's Field. The shapes of the crowded leaves on the branches of the trees form figures and faces that make you stop and wonder whether spirits planted them in order to communicate images to the living, or if they are just the products of "matrixing." Are our minds creating faces and shapes out of the environment where none really exist? Jason said he often gets these faces and shapes in his images and he believed there was more to it than mere matrixing.

The spirits at haunted sites don't always reveal themselves to strangers. Typically, the spirits don't produce any solid evidence for us to take home, possibly because it's not us they wish to communicate with. In contrast, these same spirits might often reveal themselves to the residents of these haunted houses and buildings, or to some of the visitors to the graveyards and roads that are said to be genuinely haunted, but not to others who visit. The spirits would do this for their own reasons, the likes of which we cannot ascertain, usually not even with the help of Ouija® boards or séances, both of which are of questionable value. Perhaps the spirits in these places have no interest in communicating with visitors other than the ones they select for their own reasons.

In an effort to let the spirits get to know us, Diane and I visit the places we investigate often and at all different hours of the day. This is especially valuable at graveyards where responses are more likely to take place if the investigator is persistent.

Potter's Field

Digital Dowsing

One hot, sunny day, Diane and I joined Peggy Vetrano and six members of Eastern Suffolk Paranormal (www.easternsuffolkparanormal.com) on a daytime investigation of Potter's Field. Diane and I had investigated places with Peggy in the past. A very interesting addition to this investigation was the employment of a spirit communication box — called an Ovilus — that Peggy had purchased.

The Ovilus is a hand-held, $200 electronic device that produces words through a speaker in response to "triggers" the box receives from the environment. In this instance, the voice that the Ovilus produces is male and sounds electronic rather than human. Its maker, Bill Chappell, who describes himself as a retired engineer, programmed the 512 words it is capable of producing into the device. The words in the machine can, presumably, be selected by the spirits and thus said by the box. According to the Ovilus' website, the device is "able to make phonetic speech from the immediate environment," but by what mechanism the spirits can achieve this feat is a mystery.

Surprisingly, the Ovilus' biggest skeptic is its developer, Bill Chappell, who has admitted in interviews that he is not entirely sure how spirits manipulate the pre-programmed words in the box. However, he said that many ghost hunters have reported getting messages from the dead through it. Oftentimes the one-word messages seem to have relevance to those who hear them. In other cases, people have reported the Ovilus stringing words together to form short phrases. The following experience, found on a TAPS Beyond Reality Events forum *(www.beyondrealityevents.com)*, was posted by member "OrbWithWings" on August 29, 2008:

William Sanchez and Peggy Vetrano of Eastern Suffolk Paranormal experiment with amplification of an Ovilus digital dowsing tool during an investigation of Potter's Field.

> I got the chance to play with one a little this weekend. It really was kind of freaky! The first time I used it, I had just been talking to someone about my kids and the little boy I miscarried and how I still think about him. Turned on the Ovilus about fifty feet away from where that conversation took place and it starts saying, "good mommy, brother, sister... good mother, sit rest, good mommy..." Crap!! Then down in the entrance to the cave it was saying, "granite, look, nail (when we got two steps further down the walkway, there was a nail sticking out), uncle, violent, go, dangerous" and other stuff I can't remember right now. Very VERY interesting!

On this day, Peggy was particularly interested in getting more information pertaining to two EVPs captured on voice recorders during previous investigations at Potter's Field. She wanted to use the Ovilus to see if she could find out anything more about what she had heard. In two separate EVPs, her group caught the words "Peterson's Grave" and "Hausine."

Researching the names of the people buried at Potter's Field, Peggy learned that "Peterson" and "Hausine" are the names of men buried in the graveyard. They are represented by grave markers 979 and 689 respectively. John Peterson died in 1940 at age 77, and Hausine Wadsted died in 1918 at the age of 92.

Could the names Peggy recorded in Potter's Field correspond to the men with the same names buried in the graveyard? Could it be their spirits were calling for recognition? If so, why didn't the spirits say more through the Ovilus?

The Technical Future

Readers may remember Peggy's disturbing photographs of faces on logs in the woods of Sweet Hollow Road mentioned in our book *Long Island's Most Haunted*. The likelihood that she could have captured faces on a log in the middle of the haunted woods seems as remote as capturing the voices of spirits on a voice recorder at Potter's Field, but she *did* capture faces on the log — and she *did* capture voices on her voice recorder at Potter's Field, too.

Peggy also caught a paranormal mist one night in Potter's Field (see photo) and noted that "attempts to reproduce the effect with breath were unsuccessful" because it was a paranormal mist — and *not* a mist created by someone breathing or smoking.

We have long admired Peggy's spirit photography and EVP work. Her interests in new areas of technology to reach the spirits are forward thinking and inspire Diane and I to learn more, too.

We have been fascinated by such electronic devices dating back to the first box of its kind to reach consumers, "Frank's Box," which Christopher Moon, founder of *Haunted Times Magazine*, brought to the public's attention and has exhibited for people on many occasions in recent years. One such occasion when Moon reportedly had great success with Frank's Box was during a session in the Lizzie Borden House in Fall River, Massachusetts, in the June 2009.

"Frank's Box" gained national attention when Americans saw it employed by investigators on a case on the television show, "Paranormal State." Also referred to as "The Telephone to the Dead," Frank's Box seems to mysteriously elicit messages from the "other side." Critics of the device say it is just a crude noise generator that can't possibly reach the dead. Messages are heard from Frank's Box by means of a built-in speaker.

Supposedly, its developer, Frank Sumption, fashioned the device on concepts Thomas Edison had been exploring in his efforts to develop a telephone to reach deceased persons. Schematics to build similar devices at home are available on some paranormal websites.

Was the Ovilus Successful?

So, when Peggy invited us to see if the Ovilus could make communication with Peterson or Hausine, we jumped at the chance to join her and Eastern Suffolk Paranormal in Potter's Field Cemetery. On this day we would try to expand on her group's previous work in Potter's Field. Hopefully, we would get the spirits to elaborate on "Peterson's Grave" and "Hausine" and tell us why they spoke to Peggy in her EVPs. What did they want to communicate?

Potter's Field

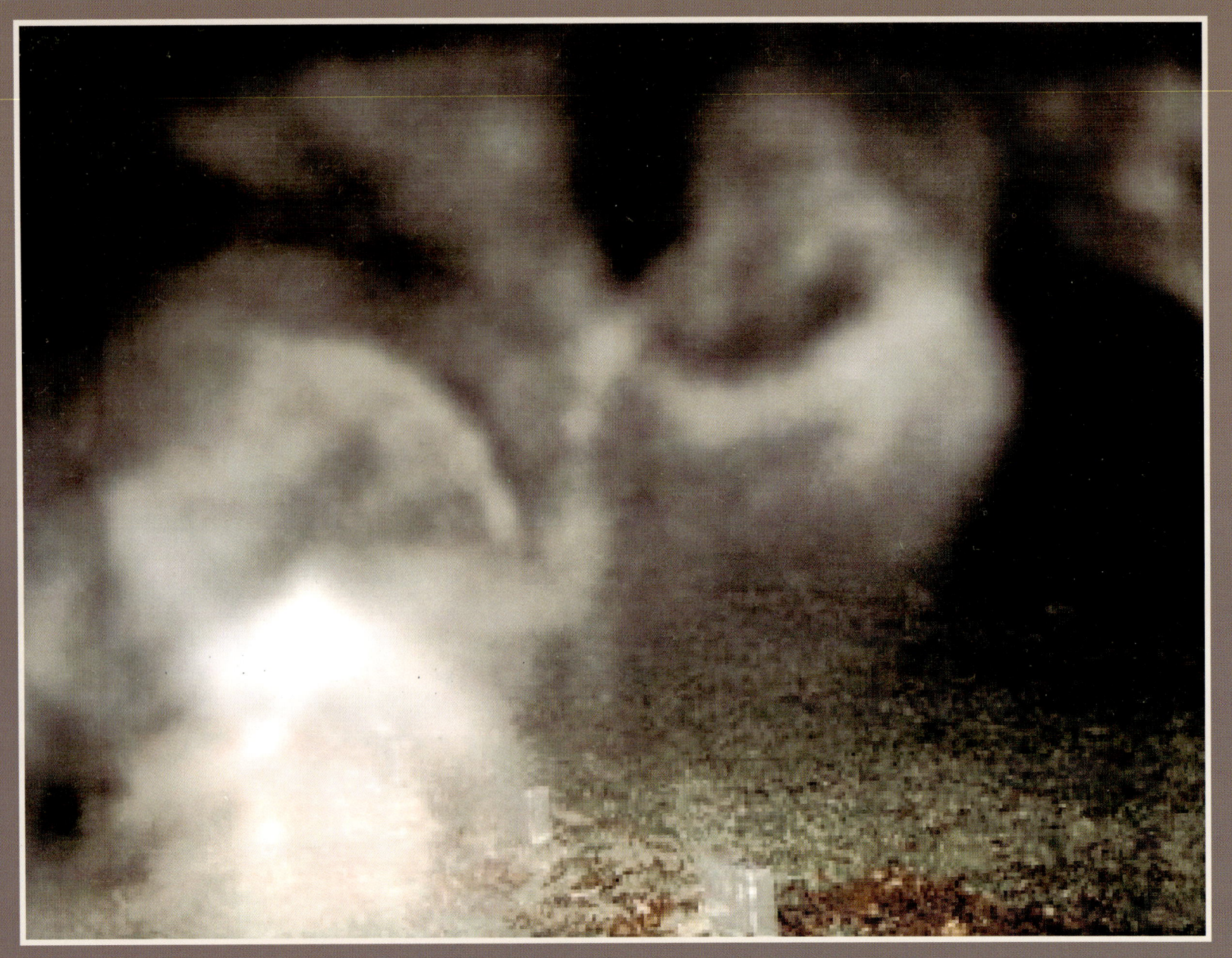

This photo of mists was taken at Potter's Field. Look closely at the upper right-side corner: Are these images of two partial ghostly faces emerging from the mist? Do you see other faces and figures in the picture? *Courtesy of Peggy Vetrano.*

Potter's Field

As we all stood under tall trees to shade us from the harsh sunlight and the 92-degree heat, we clearly heard the box say "nineteen."

The eight of us looked at each other confused and dismissed the number as irrelevant. Suddenly, Peggy broke from our circle and, pointing down at the grave in front of which we were standing, she said, "Look, Gravestone 19!"

As unbelievable as it was, she was right! Out of one thousand similar looking graves in this forgotten cemetery, we were standing in front of grave "19."

Peggy didn't get any other startling messages that hot afternoon. However, the box said "Potter's" several times at different places in the graveyard.

We wondered if this strange box had magic to it or were we all just being silly for putting any stock in it at all. Could the electronic device really pick up messages from the spirits at Potter's Field? Was the box giving the spirits a voice through which they could talk to the living?

The Ovilus has 512 words programmed into its chip. When we

Peggy Vetrano holds a device known as an Ovilus.

Potter's Field

found out that the word "Potters," along with other words we heard the machine say, are *not* words programmed into it, the source of the words caused great consternation. How could the Ovilus produce words it doesn't have stored in its memory? Did the spirits manipulate sounds, or phonemes (the smallest parts of words), already in the machine to produce their own words? If so, how did they do it?

Perhaps the scariest word Peggy ever got while using the Ovilus in Potter's Field was "Satan." It is also *not* a word programmed into the machine, so where did it come from?

During our investigation with the Ovilus, the box often said random words for which there was no obvious context or no specific circumstances at the time that should prompt such a word. Therefore, we were forced to assume that the box often produces "digital dowsing" junk.

We also noticed the more we moved, the more it spit out random words that had no apparent meaning. The box, for example, would not shut up as we walked across the graveyard. Many of the outputs were the word "No."

Users of the Ovilus across the nation have posted messages to online paranormal boards indicating they have had experiences with the machine in which words that are not programmed are produced from the gadget. Typically, these investigators express deep skepticism while also enjoying their fascination with the box.

Peggy and her group record nearly everything said on investigations with voice recorders. Back at home, the digital voice recorders are connected to computers and the recordings downloaded for study with the aid of sophisticated computer programs that help strip away noise. This is the stage when they — and most other EVP specialists — discover the ghostly voices they've captured. It was during these stud-

Paranormal investigators from Eastern Suffolk Paranormal conduct an investigation at Potter's Field.

ies of their recordings that the EVPs "Peterson's Grave" and "Hausine" were uncovered, but apparently neither Peterson nor Hausine had anything to say to us when we employed the Ovilus on that hot summer day.

In one of her investigations at Potter's Field, Peggy also caught an EVP of a woman's voice saying, "Who's talking so loudly?"

Several months later, I, too, had an experience with a woman's voice.

Joe's Experience

I was alone in Potter's Field, walking and photographing every corner and angle of the graveyard.

As I walked the forlorn property that August afternoon, I often had to fight off mosquitoes and gnats, and jump out of the way of flickering blue and brown diamond needles with long stingers that seemed to want to land on me. Small territorial birds flew overhead and swooped down close to my face as they complained in squeaks that sounded like the sonar of bats. The temperature was ninety-four degrees and the sky was dark and foreboding with the threat of an impending storm.

As I made my way into the shade of the trees on the west side of the cemetery, a woman's voice suddenly came clearly to me. The woman was humming the melody of a song that I didn't recognize.

I listened to it for many seconds before I asked, "Where are you?"

The humming stopped abruptly.

I looked around. I was alone in the graveyard.

"Do you want to tell me something?" I asked.

The humming started up again.

The woman's humming lasted for many more seconds before it simply stopped altogether. I waited around another hour for the humming to return, but it was gone.

I could barely wait until I returned to our studio to review the video I recorded. I was certain the video camera had captured the woman's humming because the entire episode occurred directly under the watchful eye of the video camera's lens. Earlier I had set the camera up high on a tripod so it would record my movements as I wandered around the cemetery.

I was right in front of the camera when the ghostly humming occurred. The Sony camera has excellent sound recording capability, so I was confident the voice recorded onto the disk in the camera.

Back at the studio, I finalized the disk, removed it from the camera, loaded it in a computer, and played the video back on a monitor. Most of the disk was fine and recorded the scenes and sounds brilliantly. Yet, when it came to the segment that should have shown the episode with the woman's voice, the disk suddenly crashed. All at once the video dragged, delayed, and stopped altogether with many seconds of time between frames, interrupting the flow of the video so that it was rendered useless.

Not giving up, I took the disk out of the computer and put it in the DVD player in my living room — the same problem revealed itself to me.

I tried several other ways to retrieve the ghostly video, but all attempts failed.

A spirit woman hummed in Potter's Field and the video camera should have recorded it, but at the exact time of the humming, the disk crashed. Was this an accident or did the spirit's energy disrupt the heads in the camera? Did the humming spirit create distortion on the disk? The problem I encountered that day with the disk had never happened before and has not happened since.

2

St. George's Church and Cemetery

Hempstead

Location: 319 Front Street, Hempstead, Nassau County, New York.

How to get there: Take the Long Island Expressway to Exit 39S Glen Cove Road. Take Glen Cove Road. Cross over Old Country Road, and continue to Clinton Road. Make a right on Front Street. Church will be on your left.

Description: St. George's Church Cemetery is wrapped around St. George's Episcopal Church and rectory. The buildings are listed on the National Registry of Historic Places.

The grave of Revolutionary War soldier Samuel Carman. Gravestones for Revolutionary War soldeirs are marked by bronze plaques, placed there by the Daughters of the American Revolution.

St. George's Church and Cemetery

Ghost Images on Gravestones

Blaring horns and traffic noises fade into the background as we step through the white gate and up the dark slate walkway approaching St. George's Episcopal Church in Hempstead. The full moon lights our path on this cool fall evening, but we are not deceived. When it comes to ghosts, all humans are in the dark.

The quaint country church appears serene in the soft glow of the moonlight. The golden rooster weathervane atop the church's tall spire shimmers against a backdrop of the glittering night sky.

Painted white with black shutters, St. George's Church is simple and quietly elegant. Tiffany & Company made several of the inspiring and brilliantly colored stained glass windows. We stopped for a moment to admire the majesty of the beautiful Georgian architecture.

As lovely as the church building is, it's the cemetery surrounding the church that commands our attention on this shadowy October night. The rustling leaves sound much like whispering spirits as we walk on the grass among the gravestones of the dead. We come as students trying to learn from those who would teach us from the other side, and so I ask, "Does anyone want to communicate with us?"

We hear a bottle roll over in the street behind a cement wall at the rear of the cemetery. A bird squawks loudly and suddenly takes flight. It casts a large shadow against the church building as it flies off into the night.

Historic St. George's Episcopal Church in Hempstead.

St. George's Church and Cemetery

This graveyard is historic. Soldiers from the Revolutionary War are buried here. Their graves bear bronze markers placed there by the Daughters of the American Revolution. *But is it haunted?*

We believe it is, but not in the usual way... There are *no* ghosts rising from the ground and hovering over this graveyard. Instead, the spirits choose to communicate in a unique way — by having their faces appear on the gravestones.

Dead Guy Face

Time and the elements have erased the name and dates off the gravestone, so we never knew his name. A psychic who saw his photograph at one of our library presentations told us his name was George, but we lovingly refer to him as "Dead Guy Face."

A light wind scrapes the red and gold leaves along the sidewalk. I step onto the grass and stand transfixed in front

Sadly, sometime after our visit there, this historic graveyard was the target of vandals. Dead Guy's gravestone was one of the casualties — it was toppled and broken. Now the only evidence we have of this spectral phenomenon is our photograph.

St. George's Church and Cemetery

Photograph of faces manifesting on a gravestone at St. George's Cemetery.

St. George's Church and Cemetery

of the grave. It is located in an area at the rear of the old church. I am awestruck by the dead face I see on its surface.

The image is clear and unmistakably visible. The face was not etched into the limestone by a stonecutter or painted on by an artist. No, instead, the image appears to be *manifesting onto the surface* through a mysterious power of its own. Paranormal forces found a way to materialize using the environment.

Dead Guy's widow's peak and nose are well-defined. His eyes are shut. His lips seem to be sewn together. This is what he may have looked like as he lay in his coffin.

He is not alone, though. Dead Guy is joined by other images on this gravestone, including a glamorous woman looking pleadingly up to heaven.

What makes this paranormal phenomenon even more amazing is that these images can easily be seen by the naked eye.

Ma and Pa Kettle

Dead Guy Face is not the only spirit in this graveyard who communicates by manifesting his image on his gravestone. We found another set of faces on a stone located in the middle of the cemetery. We nicknamed them "Ma and Pa Kettle."

An old man in a black jacket appears to be seated with his fingers laced together. An old woman with white hair appears to be lying in bed to the right side of the gentleman. Her head is cocked toward him as she looks out at the world. Perhaps this is an image of her at the instance of death. Maybe the man is her husband and he is praying for her spirit to reach heaven.

50

Could they be a couple that journeyed together though life and now continue their journey in the afterlife? Are they trying to relay a message about what lies beyond the grave?

(To view the photograph of 'Ma and Pa Kettle', go to our website and follow the link to St. George's Cemetery.)

Face on Wall

One Sunday afternoon Joe and I stopped by St. George's Cemetery to photograph the graves, hoping to capture the most elusive of ghost hunting gold — ghosts! We spoke to the spirits in friendly tones as we strolled around the neatly kept graveyard snapping photographs. I placed a voice recorder at a strategic point in the cemetery in an effort to catch disembodied voices of spirits.

Suddenly, there was a loud thud. It sounded like someone had jumped off the tall cement wall that borders the back of the graveyard, landing with a heavy thump on the grass. Joe and I quickly turned expecting to see someone behind us, but no one was there. We were alone.

It was then that we noticed flickering sunlight creeping across the wall even though the trees were still. We immediately photographed the area — and an image of a huge face on the wall was captured. Unlike the images of Dead Guy Face and Ma and Pa Kettle, the image of this face could not be seen with the naked eye.

Some people say the face looks Egyptian because the face appears to be wearing a headdress. Still others suggest the face looks like an Indian similar to those who once roamed the Hempstead plains.

(You can view this photo by visiting our website and following the link to St. George's Cemetery.)

Dorothy

Ghost investigating can be mundane and boring. It is hardly a thrill a minute. Many times we have spent hours photographing graveyards or other supposedly haunted places with not even a dust orb to show for it. It's like going fishing and not getting a single tug on the line.

We visited St. George's Cemetery one afternoon with Angel Bill, an interfaith minister and intuitive from West Hempstead; the three of us walked around the graveyard taking photographs and attempting to connect with the spirits. None of us felt any sensations or hints of activity.

Packing up our equipment, we headed back to my SUV and left. I was driving, Angel Bill was in the passenger seat, and Joe was in the backseat. Joe said he felt there was a spirit present. He said he was experiencing a sickly feeling in his chest that he associated with a spirit's presence. He felt paranormal cobwebs drifting across his face and hands. He said the hair on the back of his neck was standing up and the air felt dense all around him.

He began shooting photographs.

We arrived home and headed up to my studio. There we downloaded the photographs we had just taken at St. George's Cemetery. We studied them closely. Nothing unusual appeared in the graveyard photographs, but the photos shot in the SUV told another story.

Joe captured the gentle face of a woman in the side view mirror on the passenger side of the vehicle. I looked at the photo and immediately said to Joe, "Her name is Dorothy."

"How do you know that?" he asked, surprised.

"I just know," I answered.

I am not at all psychic, but for some unexplainable reason, I knew I was right. Joe seemed to feel I was right too, but like me, he couldn't explain why he felt that way. *(The photo can be viewed on our website.)*

Dorothy's spirit stayed with us for a couple of months. She did playful things to let us know she was around.

One morning, I was rushing off to work and couldn't find my keys. I was positive I dropped them on the couch next to my purse, but they weren't there. I searched everywhere, but my keys were nowhere to be found. As I passed through the living room again, I saw the keys lying on the couch — right next to my purse! They hadn't been there a moment earlier when I searched. Since I was home alone, no one could have been playing tricks on me. No one that is except for our playful spirit, Dorothy!

Then there was the time when Joe woke up to find that he had no heat. It was the middle of January and the days were frigid. He thought his furnace malfunctioned in the middle of the night. On his shivering way to the basement, he stopped to check the thermostat. It had been turned all the way off! Joe lives alone and the thermostat dial is located in a place where it's nearly impossible to knock into it or accidentally turn the dial to shut the heat off. Joe was convinced Dorothy was having a little fun with him.

Perhaps the most convincing sign of Dorothy's presence was on an evening when Joe and I were sitting at his kitchen table writing an article for a newspaper. We were laughing. When we stopped, a woman's laughter erupted loudly right beside us. The disembodied laughter scared us so badly we both jumped. We looked at each other as we regained our composure and simultaneously said, "Dorothy!"

It was difficult getting to sleep that night. The house seemed alive with foreign noises, banging, and shrieks. We had only just fallen asleep when we were simultaneously awakened by a very bright flash of light. It was so bright it reminded me of the grand finale at a Grucci fireworks extravaganza. Shortly after that night's remarkable display, Dorothy's spirit seemingly vanished from our lives — or so we thought.

The Victorian House Connection

Two years later, Joe and I were invited to investigate a lovely old Victorian house on Suffolk's South Shore along with several other paranormal investigators. Most times when we conduct investigations, Joe and I go in separate directions. Joe uses the video camera while I take photographs. This time was no different. We split up as soon as we entered the house. I went upstairs while Joe roamed around on the main floor.

Joe was in the dining room, where he kept zooming in on the photograph of a woman in a frame displayed on the table. If he wandered away from the photograph and shot video of other things, he'd soon come back to the photo and zoom in on it.

"I was drawn to it," he'd later tell me.

When I entered the dining room, I noticed the same photograph — and I was also drawn to it. The woman looked so familiar. I knew her from somewhere, but where?

Joe and I went down into the basement. The homeowner was there with two other investigators. He was showing them items that belonged to his mother who had passed away several years before.

"Who is the woman in the photograph on the dining room table?" I asked.

"That's my mother," the man answered.

"What was her name?"

"Dorothy...Dotty," the homeowner replied.

Joe and I looked at each other in amazement. The photograph he took in the side view mirror outside St. George's

A photograph on the dining room table of a haunted house. The woman in the photograph had a striking resemblance to the woman's face we photographed in a side view mirror of our vehicle at St. George's Cemetery two years earlier.

Cemetery in Hempstead nearly two years earlier looked like this man's mother!

Although we were excited, neither of us said a word just then. When we got out of the house, we exploded and talked about it all the way home.

We called the homeowner a couple of days later and asked if we could come over and show him a photograph. We downloaded Dorothy's photo onto a disk and returned to the old Victorian. Once the homeowner brought the photo up on his computer, I asked him, "Does she look familiar?"

"It's my mother when she was younger!" the man immediately responded.

When we told him about our experiences with Dorothy's ghost, he wasn't surprised. He told us his mother's spirit is often around him. "My mom had a great sense of humor…she loved to laugh," he said.

What makes this story even more puzzling is that although Dorothy's spirit attached itself to us at St. George's Cemetery, she is not buried there nor did she have any connection to the church.

We told our story and showed the photo of Dorothy's ghost at a presentation we gave at the Hampton Bays Public Library a few years ago. A woman from the audience came up to us afterward and told us she knew Dorothy and took care of her before she died.

Dorothy had found a unique way to communicate with her son and her caretaker from the other side. It is our belief that many times spirits come back to say, "I love you." We are grateful Dorothy chose us to deliver the messages.

The spirits of St. George's Cemetery found a gentle way to make their presence known. For those of you who are frightened at the thought of seeing or being touched by a ghost, we suggest an afternoon visit to this historic graveyard so you can experience the paranormal without being scared to death.

A woman's face appeared to the camera in the sideview mirror of our vehicle as we pulled away from St. George's Cemetery.

3
East Hillside Cemetery
Glen Head

Location: Junction of Glen Cove Road and Route 107, Glen Head, New York.

Description: Colonial cemetery on a hill with over five hundred graves; the oldest grave dates back to 1790.

How to get there: Take the Long Island Expressway to Exit 41N (Routes 106-107) and bear left at fork to 107. Continue north at junction of 107 and Glen Cove Road. The cemetery will be on the right.

Entrance to East Hillside Cemetery.

Is East Hillside Cemetery patrolled by guardian spirits?

East Hillside Cemetery

A paranormal mist shaped like a face watches as we photograph the graveyard.

Guardian Spirits?

The awful event started with a harrowing voice ripping through the godforsaken night from somewhere deep amid the sea of ancient gravestones down the old crooked hill: "Bradley's been hurt!"

Coincidentally, at that very moment, the night was on fire with paranormal activity.

East Hillside Cemetery was popping with spirits, but not all of them were good, we'd soon be told.

Ghost lights and orbs, tracked by infrared video and still photography, flew across the grounds and whirled around a bat-infested tree wherein bats squealed at us, carrying our imaginations off to the edge of vampire realities.

Shadows moved across the graveyard where no shadows should have moved at all.

Ghost mists rose out of graves — *into our photographs* — and across the sky. Some of these ecto-mists were seen even without the aid of cameras.

Spirits surrounded us with their toxic presence. Their close proximity crawled on our skin and up the

East Hillside Cemetery

Young boy fending off ghosts at East Hillside. *Drawing by Karen Isaksen.*

East Hillside Cemetery

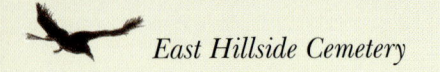

back of our necks to the crest of our heads and then melted into the sides of our faces like fingers bleeding into our flesh.

The spirits cast paranormal cobwebs across our eyes, noses, and mouths — and impregnated our chests with the heavy sickly feelings of their deaths.

Ghost hunter Cyndi Philbin of Kings Park said she felt something touch her face near her mouth. No one was surprised.

A few moments later people said they smelled the scent of old cigars in the air. This is a common smell whiffed when spirits are around.

Ghosts were everywhere around us and nowhere around us at the same time.

Just then an investigator emerged out of the darkness and stood breathlessly before me.

"Bradley has been attacked by a spirit!" the investigator exclaimed, panting from running up the steep hill.

"What do you mean, attacked?" I demanded.

A mist, some people say looks like a face, rises from the ground beside ghost investigator Cyndi Philbin in East Hillside Cemetery at night.

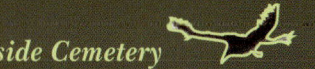

East Hillside Cemetery

East Hillside Cemetery

"He was punched in the abdomen. He's really hurt!"

"Who punched him?"

"That's the thing: Bradley was alone!" said the investigator. "There was nobody there who could have punched him. He says a ghost did it!"

While I processed this bizarre information, I looked at my camera's LCD screen to review the photo I had taken only seconds earlier. On the screen, a white mist shaped like a hungry hellhound hung in the air.

"Bradley is only ten years old," I thought. "Why would a spirit hit him?"

Though Diane and I have had many memorable nights with the powerful spirits of East Hillside Cemetery — whom I think of as the graveyard's Guardians — it is the bleak full moon night that young Bradley was allegedly assaulted by an entity that we, with great regret, remember mostly.

Bradley was only a child. He stood before us on the crest of the hill in the dark of the cemetery. He pulled open his coat and then pulled up his shirt — on his abdomen was a large round red spot. It was identical to the blotch a human hand would have left if it whacked Bradley square in the stomach. I shone my flashlight on the mark and sucked in my breath.

"Something slapped me," Bradley started in shuddering whimpers, wiping his wet eyes with his pudgy fingers, bouncing up and down on the toes of his sneakers in the grips of barely controllable anxiety.

"Who did that to you?"

Mist in the shape of a hellhound appears during a haunted night at East Hillside Cemetery.

East Hillside Cemetery

"Nobody!" Bradley answered through a flood of tears. "Nobody was there! I was alone! Something just hit me!"

He began crying anew with the remembrance of the alleged unholy violence against him.

Even as the traumatized boy cried, his eyes maintained a darting vigilance for ghosts lurking at the edge of darkness. He jumped nervously in reaction to quick or unexpected movements made by the ghost hunters around him.

"Nobody was there!" he muttered again, looking with frightened eyes around at the moonlit graves.

After he spoke the words, I turned away from the circle that had gathered around him to find a place to put down the camera bag, which I had up to then carried by a strap hanging

Joe photographed a light anomaly in the sky right above the whole ghost hunting group, but nobody saw it with their naked eyes. It looked like a Fourth of July "helicopter" firework.

over my shoulder. When Bradley saw me suddenly reappear from out of the darkness to rejoin the circle, he screamed, thinking I was a ghost.

"I'm not dead yet!" I said to him, trying to raise a smile, but it didn't work. There was no way to console the terrorized youth.

Bradley was one of four children on our ghost hunt this night. His mother, aunt, and their four children joined about ten of us for the East Hillside outing. Our ghost investigation group had no age restrictions for attendees to hunts, provided minors had a parent present.

All four children were well-behaved and lovable. They had been on several prior ghost hunts with us. Never had an occurrence taken place such as the one Bradley experienced tonight.

The graveyard at night. *Drawing by Karen Isaksen.*

On hunts the adults often joked and talked with the children, and sometimes we told ghost stories while sitting in a wide circle on the grass in the dark of night in a cemetery at the conclusion of a hunt. The adults were happy to have the children join us, and sometimes we all went out to eat together after an outing.

Up until then, ghost hunting had been a harmless and fun activity for Bradley, his sister, and their two cousins. Who would have ever guessed a spirit in East Hillside Cemetery would attack a child? The notion was unthinkable!

Bradley's mother removed her son from the graveyard and took him home shortly after he showed people the mark left on his abdomen from what he claimed was an attack by an unseen entity. The rest of us went distractedly back to ghost hunting when Bradley departed. We quickly found ourselves fully engrossed in our ongoing activities, for the spirits were with us tonight and we had to document signs of what we believed was their presence.

We were all hoping to capture a photograph of the apparition that supposedly had hit the boy — if there was such an apparition lurking among us. What was it? Who was it? Why was it?

There was no apparition, though, as we only captured mists in our photos and video. We photographed flying orbs, ghost lights, and bats swooping down next to our heads and fluttering their erratic wings before tearing away into the spooky silvery moonlit night. We caught EMF spikes and felt sensations we believed were inspired by the spirits' close presence or resulted from them touching us.

Was the alleged ghost attack all in Bradley's imagination? Had he run into the edge of a grave or walked into a pole that jabbed him in the stomach? Several of us searched the area where he claimed to have been struck by an ill-tempered ghost,

East Hillside Cemetery

Machpelah Cemetery in Ridgewood, Queens.

but we didn't find anything sticking out from a grave into which the boy could have walked.

Certainly, there were bushes on the grounds that he could have banged into and mistaken for a hand, but a collision with a branch of a bush would have scratched his skin and left distinct marks.

Mike Salvia, an experienced and well known paranormal investigator from Old Bethpage, aimed his video camera at Bradley at one point before the boy left the graveyard to go home and asked, "What did it feel like when you got hit?"

"It felt like I was going to fall down," he said.

Then Bradley told me during my interview with him that he felt he had been pursued in the graveyard. He was confident he had not walked into something, but that *something* hit him.

This night Mike Salvia was shooting footage with his Sony video camera set on Nightshot infrared. He employed a separate infrared illuminator affixed to the top of the camera. This equipment enabled him to see far into the dark of night. The eyes of the ghost hunters looked demonic. Everything was tinged green from the effect of the infrared.

East Hillside Cemetery

If there's anybody on Long Island who has an understanding of paranormal activity, it's Mike Salvia, who lived in a haunted house in Huntington where he regularly saw ghosts and other paranormal activity. He has photographed many forms of spirit manifestations, including apparitions on Sweet Hollow Road in Melville. He is a man with an uncanny talent for capturing spirit activity on video and in still photos.

He also senses the spirits.

Mike stood with us in the cemetery where we had gathered in a loose circle with Bradley. His video recorder was on and captured what he had said to Bradley's mother.

> "Nobody wants to think a spirit would do something like hit a child, but there are bad spirits out there…just like there are bad people. I am not familiar with this cemetery being bad like that!"

Salvia paused to consider a thought.

> "You know, at the very second when they said Bradley got hit, I was getting all these orbs in my pictures and I was feeling an angriness — not like a raving mad lunatic angriness — but a feeling like the spirits were upset, like they were asking, 'Why are you here?'"

This unfortunate night at East Hillside would end Bradley's participation in our group ghost hunts, as Bradley's mother and her sister dropped out of the group. The children would not visit graveyards with us again — and for that we were sorry. They had added a vitality to our hunts that was missed afterwards.

Opposite: This is the cemetery where Harry Houdini is buried. Was it a man or an apparition in a long-sleeve white shirt that sat before the broken window in the tower of the boarded-up building?

An Unfriendly Place at Night

In our opinion, East Hillside is hands down the most unfriendly of the haunted graveyards on Long Island. This might have something to do with Hessian soldiers from Germany buried in unmarked graves on the property during the American Revolution. They were the enemies of the Patriots, and as hired mercenaries, killed Americans for a paycheck from the British.

While we consider Machpelah Cemetery in Ridgewood Queens — where Harry Houdini is buried — the creepiest and most mysterious cemetery on Long Island, it is East Hillside we believe is the most spiritually troubled cemetery we have come across so far. Machpelah Cemetery, located on Cypress Hills Road in Ridgewood, evokes feelings of being watched and studied by entities. In contrast, East Hillside radiates for us a feeling of being pursued.

In Machpelah, we recorded on video a white-faced phantom hiding in the darkness of the shadows beside a building. The phantom scared a bird with its sudden appearance. The bird flew quickly out of the area in squawking complaint.

We also photographed at Machpelah the apparition of a man in a window of a boarded up old building staring absently down at us without moving. He appeared to be sitting in a chair. The building's windows were broken and barbed wire kept people away. The apparition watched us with a blank stare while we studied him in the rectangle of the window. Then he watched us as we inspected the rest of the desolate building. The man appeared to be wearing a long-sleeved white shirt — the kind Houdini used to wear. Houdini's gravesite is located only yards away from the building.

In contrast, East Hillside Cemetery produces walls of ecto-mist at night that are so overwhelming they make us feel uncomfortable — *even in danger* — as though the mist will overtake us or turn into something that will.

East Hillside Cemetery

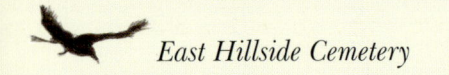

It's our opinion that at night, East Hillside becomes an unsettled territory. The spirits there do not radiate a welcoming feeling to ghost hunters. If you ask us, we'd have to say that the dead of the graveyard don't want ghost hunters poking around on their property after dark. Guardian spirits seem to be protecting the grounds.

It's that simple.

According to historians, several Hessian soldiers from Germany, hired by the British as mercenaries to fight the patriots during the American Revolution, succumbed to smallpox while on Long Island and were buried in unmarked graves in East Hillside. The unsettled spirits in this graveyard — if there are any — might be the result of angry foreign mercenaries who died on their enemy's land far away from home. Certainly there is something about this cemetery that distinguishes it from others on Long Island.

The truth is this is a graveyard that should be skipped by ghost hunters because we feel things have the potential to go awry here quickly. We will tell you about this place because it's our job, but it's our hope you visit this cemetery only during the day and forsake it at night.

An additional problem that should ward off ghost hunters from visiting this place at night is that the local police will swoop down upon you like hawks if you're in the graveyard on a ghost hunt after dark. They are well-informed about ghost hunting activities in this cemetery and they are prepared to find you.

However, if the police don't get you, tripping over a stone in the dangerous nighttime environment just might — and if you miraculously manage to avoid both the police and the potential harm of the dangers of the nighttime environment, perhaps it will be a spirit that gets you. As you now know, a spirit attack on a human has been alleged to have happened in East Hillside Cemetery before.

The Police

The local police do not tolerate nighttime visitors to East Hillside Cemetery. Officers in patrol cars arrive within minutes of the first flashes of cameras.

A ghostly mist looms over Diane after she accidentally steps into the soft earth of a recently filled-in grave. Look in the very center of the photo: do you see a face occupying a large area above and to the left of Diane? This face and the paranormal mist followed Diane around the graveyard.

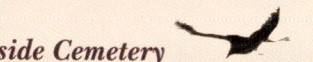

East Hillside Cemetery

East Hillside Cemetery

Upon revisiting the same grave a few weeks later, a mist immediately appeared around Diane in the area of the gravesite she had stepped into — as if it remembered her. These two photographs and the following two photographs (on opposite page) show the progression of the mist that seemed to observe us for a brief period. Though it remained mostly in this area, the mist did follow us into the middle of the cemetery before vanishing.

Ghost hunters might consider this unfair. After all, there aren't any signs posted with strict hours for visiting the graveyard and there are no gates keeping people out. The open driveway and the stairs ascending from the street seem to invite anyone who wishes to enter day or night.

On the night we were *busted* there, the officers told us they didn't want people in the graveyard after dark chiefly because their department receives phone calls from nearby residents worried that the flashing camera lights are thieves with flashlights using the cemetery as a means of accessing private backyards to burglarize homes. This might explain why the police tend to be so quick in their arrival when ghost hunters are in the graveyard at night.

While in our experiences the police officers from the local municipality were fairly polite, they are also highly efficient and don't miss a trick. For a ghost hunter this can interpret into a night in jail if there are any legal skeletons in the closet.

Diane and I were once at East Hillside at night with Mike Salvia when police officers drove up the driveway and shined their bright spotlight on our vehicles parked by a building at the top of the grounds. We had arrived in two cars only a few minutes earlier to do some spirit photography. We shone our flashlights up at the officers from down the hill and shouted to them that we were coming up the hill to explain ourselves.

Once at our vehicles, the officers made us hand over our licenses, and they shined their flashlights inside our vehicles. They checked the registration and inspection stickers. They made us stand beside our cars while they asked us questions with their flashlight beams in our eyes.

One officer stood guardedly in front of us, watching our every move, asking us questions while his hand readied the draw of his pistol if needed. Meanwhile, the other officer talked over the car radio to headquarters as the dispatcher ran our licenses to see if there were any warrants out for us.

I wanted to avoid telling the cops we were ghost hunters for fear they would want to make examples of us by locking us up, so I told them some other reason why we were photographing graves in the middle of the night.

The officer standing in front of us saw right through my phony story and said, "I've been in this business a lot of years, and I found it's always best to just tell the truth."

That's it! He had me!

Diane and Mike both frowned at me and explained to the officer what we were really doing there — ghost hunting — and pled their case, asking what the big deal was about being in a graveyard where there were no signs saying stay out and no gates to keep us out. By the way, they later chastised me for creating a cover story.

East Hillside Cemetery

Look at the lower left area of this photograph: Large, white, worm-like anomalies appear to be floating above the ground. On closer inspection, you will see these anomalies are not plants or flowers. In fact, they are not even attached to the ground.

The officer standing in front of us shrugged indifferently. It was obvious arguing our common sense reasons for being there held no weight with him. He was in charge and we had to go along for the ride. Of course, the police let us off that night, but I don't ever want to meet up with these cops again in East Hillside Cemetery.

In summary, we suggest visiting this cemetery only during the daylight, lest you draw police trouble or get hurt — from something or other.

The Dead

Though it had been at least twenty-four hours since the storm, the ground at East Hillside Cemetery was soft. Diane walked ahead of me into the quiet property. Her sneakers made a squishing sound with each step. Suddenly she let out a little scream. I snapped a photograph of her at that exact moment, purely by chance. Her foot sank up to her ankle into the soil of a new grave. When I looked over the camera as I took the photograph, the flash illuminated a gigantic mist looming all around her.

Diane yanked her foot out of the mud.

"It's just like quicksand," she said, her voice quivering. "It felt as though I was being pulled down!"

For the next ten minutes, the mist stayed with Diane. It followed her as she walked through the cemetery. I photographed it many times before it disappeared altogether.

The Mist

I shot at least a hundred photos of other parts of the cemetery on this summer's night and there were no mists at all.

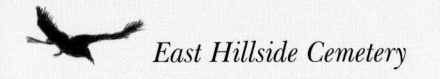

They appeared only after Diane stepped in the grave — and they stayed with her only in that section of the cemetery.

I remember snapping a photo of her and unexpectedly seeing the shape of the mist towering directly over me in the summer night, so close to me that it seemed to be leaning toward my face from only a foot away. It was perhaps twelve feet tall and wide. It extended from the ground. I jumped in reaction and quickly removed myself from the immediate area. This took place during the time I was photographing the mist around Diane. Having stepped only a few yards away from the spot, I then turned and saw in the next flash of light from my camera that the mist was now next to Diane.

On this night we had come to the cemetery to do EVP work at the grave of a young man named Kevin who was killed in the World Trade Center terrorist attack of September 11, 2001. As he was a friend of Diane's son, Diane had known him personally.

We were looking for Kevin's grave when a police car pulled into the cemetery's driveway from the road and drove slowly up the hill with the high beams and spotlight lighting up the grounds. The officer in the patrol car was looking for people in the cemetery. He must have received a call from a local resident who saw our camera flashes.

Diane's Tale

I went to East Hillside that evening with one thought in mind. I wanted to conduct an EVP session at the gravesite of my son Chuck's good friend, Kevin. It was something I felt compelled to do ever since I discovered he was buried there.

I discovered Kevin was buried there by accident — or maybe it was fate. Joe and I were visiting Mike Salvia's apartment in Old Bethpage. He was showing us photographs he had taken the night of our group ghost hunt at East Hillside Cemetery, the same night that a ghost allegedly struck Bradley.

Mike focused on a photograph that had nothing remarkable or paranormal in it, so I barely glanced at it, but he kept the photograph on the computer screen and talked about how "Kevin" was a victim of 9/11. Suddenly I realized it was the grave of my son's friend. I was awestruck. I had known Kevin since he was a little boy, and I was devastated when he was so senselessly killed.

The police car silently made its way up the narrow cemetery driveway. "Damn," I said to myself, "someone must have seen our camera flashes and called the police."

I scanned the sea of graves in the darkness looking for Joe, who was deeper in the cemetery.

"Where are you?" I called urgently, my voice just above a whisper. "The police are here!"

I was in an open area when suddenly the officer's powerful spotlight illuminated the section of the graveyard where I was standing. The brilliant light blinded me. I froze like a deer caught in headlights… I was busted!

Pocketing my voice recorder, I started up the incline toward the parking area where the police car waited, its spotlight centered on me. I hadn't taken more than three steps when, to my disbelief, the spotlight moved off me to another section of the cemetery! It was then I realized for some unexplainable reason, the police officer never even saw me!

For the officer not to have seen me was a miracle! I was walking right in front of his patrol car, but I was not about to question this unexpected gift.

I did an about face and walked down the hill to a mausoleum. Joe had been hiding there and calling to me in a sort of shouted whisper the whole time. We waited out the police search together behind the wall. The spotlight fell on the mausoleum a few times, but just in glancing, and then moved off.

We couldn't help but talk in excited whispers as we stood in the dark behind the building while the spotlight lit up the mausoleum, and moved on, and then flooded the building again, and moved on. It was like a scene from a movie about a prison break. We had to laugh about the ridiculousness of what we were doing and express amazement to each about how the officer did not see me.

We kept out of sight until the spotlight vanished and the police car exited the cemetery about ten minutes later.

Not wanting to push our luck, we hurried to the cemetery exit and flew down the cement steps. We rushed across the street to the parking lot where Joe had left his SUV.

I had just snapped on my seatbelt, and Joe was just dropping a couple of camera bags into the backseat when the police car suddenly pulled up behind us.

Joe eyed the patrol car, closed the back door, gulped, got in the vehicle, and glanced into the rearview mirror waiting for the officer to get out of his car and approach him. We didn't realize we were holding our breath until, astonishingly, the patrol car backed up and took off into the inky night!

"Looks like lightning struck twice tonight," I said. "That was so close!"

As we pulled away from the parking lot, I saw the police car reappear behind us from a side road. The car followed us out of the area. The officer tailed us for about a mile. It was then that we realized the officer was letting us know he was aware we had been in the graveyard, but he was letting us get away because he never actually saw us inside the property.

We felt it was a common sense decision on the officer's part, since it would have just wasted his time and ours. We weren't vandals, and he knew it. We were thankful he chose to let us go, bless his wise soul.

"I still can't believe that cop didn't see you," Joe said as we drove out of town. "That spotlight lit up the graveyard like it was the middle of the day!"

"Well, maybe I was invisible," I said thoughtfully.

"What do you mean?" Joe asked.

"When the spotlight hit me, I was out in the open. There was no place to hide. The cop would have been blind not to see me. Maybe Kevin's spirit surrounded me... you know, like a paranormal wall, so the cop couldn't see me. It was as though Kevin was protecting me."

"But why?" Joe wanted to know.

"Because Kevin was a sweetheart and maybe he thought he'd save Chuck the embarrassment of having to bail his crazy ghost hunting mother out of jail!"

4

Lake Ronkonkoma Cemetery

Lake Ronkonkoma

Location: On the west side of Hawkins Avenue, Lake Ronkonkoma Cemetery is just north of the "five corners."

Description: Several acres of graves on flat land in a residential neighborhood.

How to get there: Take the Long Island Expressway to Exit 60 North (Ronkonkoma Avenue). Stay on Ronkonkoma Avenue past Portion Road until it merges into Hawkins Avenue. The cemetery is on the left side (west) of Hawkins Avenue, about a quarter mile past the five corners.

Lake Ronkonkoma Cemetery.

Lake Ronkonkoma Cemetery

The Visitation

The night started slowly. Diane and I walked the grounds, talking to the spirits, and then we went our separate ways, as we usually do. It was a mild night with a refreshing breeze blowing out of the north.

Then something amazing happened.

About an hour into our investigation, as I looked through the viewfinder of my camera to line up a shot of some graves, I noticed Diane approaching me. I didn't think anything of it. At that second, I was aiming my camera at an area of the graveyard where it was dark and where in the past we had detected paranormal activity.

This was a graveyard where Diane and I had many unusual experiences, including discovering a freshly decapitated chicken that had probably been used in a Santeria curse-cleansing ritual. It led to an investigation by the Suffolk County Police Department, but that's another story.

"How's it going?" I asked.

I heard her footsteps walking up to me and I heard her stop beside me. In my peripheral vision I saw the dark image of Diane in her black pea coat standing beside me. I heard her breathing.

She didn't answer, so after I took the picture, I turned to her… She wasn't there! Nobody was!

Across the graveyard I saw the light of Diane's camera suddenly illuminate a large area of graves. My chest tightened and I felt tingles climb my spine and radiate through the top of my head. A paranormal event had just taken place and my body was thrown into alarm mode. I looked around the cemetery, fighting for composure.

It is the trauma caused by this exact kind of event — *the shock of seeing a ghost* — that has been reported over the ages as being responsible for people having their hair turning white, going deaf, dumb, blind, insane, or even being "scared to death" on the spot. The sudden appearance of ghosts runs counter to what we humans know to be normal about our reality.

A white misty mass appeared to Joe seconds after he saw a ghost in Lake Ronkonkoma Cemetery.

A mist shaped as a face with a bushy mustache looms over the graves as Joe and Diane investigate the cemetery.

A mist whirls away from Joe and into the night.

Lake Ronkonkoma Cemetery

Three light anomalies fly through Lake Ronkonkoma Cemetery in a line.

Lake Ronkonkoma Cemetery

Scientists say humans do not work off instinct, but reacting to a ghost must certainly be instinctual. The existence of ghosts has likely run side-by-side with the existence of humans from the moment our species became aware. Ghosts are part of our oldest existence. Certainly reacting to them is instinctual.

At that instant, a white form, appearing solid, came between my face and the camera that I held two feet out in front of me, and I jumped back in reaction.

Before me was a thick ectoplasmic form. I clicked my camera and saw in the viewfinder a large white mass floating right beside me. It was not my breath. It was too warm and dry for my breath to create a mist. I would dismiss a breath mist. I know the difference.

No, this was something else.

As I watched, the ecto-mist took on the form of a face with a bushy mustache and then whirled away into the oblivion of night and the unknown.

A mysterious light anomaly floats over the graves at Lake Ronkonkoma Cemetery.

What's My Name?

The event was eerily reminiscent of an extraordinary paranormal experience I had when Diane and I joined members of the Berkshire Paranormal Group in a nighttime investigation of the Hoosac Train Tunnel in North Adams, Massachusetts, in 2006. Karen Isaksen, a sensitive, of Bay Shore was with us.

About ten of us drove into the woods to visit the train tunnel. It bores four miles through the middle of a mountain. Two hundred men died while constructing the tunnel. They were mostly Irish immigrants.

As we were walking the half-mile along the tracks to reach the dark tunnel, I saw a fellow investigator with whom I had not been introduced. I turned to the person and said, "Hello, my name is Kevin." The name rolled off my tongue ever so naturally.

Of course, Kevin is *not* my name. My name is Joe. I had never in my life made a mistake about my name and it has not happened since. Even as I said the name "Kevin," I was aware it was wrong, but it was as if I had no choice but to say the name.

Karen Isaksen was behind me at that moment and she immediately told me that at the instant when I said my name was Kevin a white figure was standing beside me. "It appeared and vanished," she said.

When we got inside the train tunnel, we heard the distant screams of men. The dead were letting us know they were still there, so I'm left to wonder: Had a dead man spoken through me that night?

Did You See That?

Now, three years later in Lake Ronkonkoma Cemetery, the distinct feeling of having been visited up close and personal by a ghost overtook me once again. What was *it* that I saw? Or maybe the real question I should ask is, Who was *it* that I saw?

Whatever it was — *whomever it was* — came so close to my face I felt the wind of its presence brush by me. I continued to photograph as my heart raced. In none of the subsequent photographs did I capture anything more of this ghost of the *haunting type*.

When I went over to Diane to tell her what had happened to me, she immediately fired off two questions that confirmed *something* had been standing beside me.

Before I had the chance to tell her what I experienced, Diane asked, "Who was that who was with you? Who were you talking to?"

"Those are good questions," I answered. "I think I just saw a ghost!"

Opposite: Mists and orbs hover over the landscape of Lake Ronkonkoma Cemetery.

Lake Ronkonkoma Cemetery

5

Union Cemetery
Middle Island

Location: Union Cemetery is on the south side of Middle Country Road (State Route 25), opposite Christian Fellowship Church in Middle Island.

Description: This cemetery sits on six flat acres of land. The oldest graves are located in the northeastern section of the cemetery. However, old graves are mixed in with newer throughout the cemetery. A wrought iron archway announces "Union Cemetery" and under it begins a rutted paved road that circles the interior.

How to get there: Take Exit 66 North from the Long Island Expressway, Follow the road north some miles to Route 25 (Middle Country Road), a major intersection. Make a left turn onto Route 25 and go down about a mile. The cemetery is on the left hand side. Look for the archway across from a church.

Entrance to Union Cemetery in Middle Island.

Union Cemetery

Graves in haunted Union Cemetery.

Union Cemetery

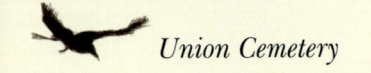

The School of Hard Knocks and Apparitions

Two experienced paranormal investigators simultaneously witnessed a ghost one silvery moonlit night in Union Cemetery in Middle Island.

Could the ghost have been the White Lady that local lore says people see hitch-hiking in front of the foreboding graveyard on dark and foggy nights only to disappear when drivers pull over to give her a ride?

"What happened was all of a sudden when the light flashed within the camera's focus there was a woman standing next to the tree wearing a long skirt," began Peggy Vetrano of Southampton.

Peggy, a well-known ghost hunter from the paranormal investigation group Eastern Suffolk Paranormal (ESP), relayed her gripping tale of the supernatural to our video camera only fifteen minutes after the spirit appeared to her and Denise Krapf, a fellow ESP paranormal researcher from Selden.

Meanwhile, the story of the White Lady of Union Cemetery has been circulating for decades among local folks, but not until this night, however, have any Long Island paranormal investigators had reason to believe the story could be true!

A ghostly woman stands next to a haunted tree.
Drawing by Karen Isaksen.

Union Cemetery

The Legend

According to the legend, a woman appears in car headlights, wan and white, on dreary foggy nights, usually during the witching hour of 2 and 3 a.m. when the veil between the worlds is believed to be its thinnest, but only to drivers who are alone and when no one else is on the road.

Alarmed by the Lady's unnatural ghostly glow and detached dead demeanor, many drivers wisely step on the gas and keep going when they spot her hitchhiking on the eastbound side of Route 25. However, some drivers will pull over to help the woman, thinking she is stranded in the night. Perhaps in the dark these drivers didn't see the White

Above: The mysterious hitchhiking White Lady of Union Cemetery.

Right: Unsettled spirits linger at the cemetery. *Drawings by Karen Isaksen.*

Union Cemetery

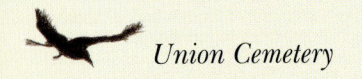

Lady's void eyes or empty dead expression, or even the unearthly pale aura she radiates.

That's the point when drivers find the sleight-of-hand of the paranormal has struck their lives at Union Cemetery. For when the drivers turn back or look in their rearview mirrors to see if the Lady is approaching their idling cars to get in the passenger door, there is suddenly no sign her. Poof! She disappears without a trace back into the world of ghastly night shadows and lonely graves inside the cemetery.

In Peggy's and Denise's case, the ghostly woman did not appear on the side of the road, but beside a tree near a crossroads at the rear of the cemetery.

While the women were relating their haunting experience to us so we could document the story on video, other paranormal investigators combed through the field of graves in the shallow light of the moon looking for more signs of paranormal activity. About a dozen people attended this September 13th ghost hunt, but like the rest of us, in their imaginations, with the haunting only minutes past, Peggy and Denise no doubt were a million miles away with thoughts of where the ghost had gone and when it would reveal itself again. Would she come back tonight?

Meanwhile, fellow investigators tread guardedly as they fanned out across the grounds like soldiers on a midnight mission. They spied each suspicious movement of the apish shadows swaggering hauntingly in the breeze under the shaggy limbs of towering pine trees in this 260-year-old graveyard. Their tools: cameras, voice recorders, and EMF detectors.

The unfamiliar quality of the hollow moonlight on the stones inspired recollections of scenes from the first lunar moonwalk where the foreign gray landscape was a place where anything could jump out of from behind the next strange rock, including ghosts.

The infamous White Lady of Union Cemetery appears to lonely drivers on Route 25 during the bewitching hour. Drawing by Karen Isaksen.

The blue-tinted light fell hazy from the sky like introspective stage lighting. The stage, in this case, was a sleeping field old dark gravestones seemingly growing wildly out the terrain like a monster's mangled teeth.

The scene could have been a Hollywood set built for a Stephen King horror movie about long-nailed ghouls with black tongues that claw their way out of rotted coffins and then through the dirt of their own grave plots. But the stark reality was much less inviting: this place was where real dead people filled the hallowed ground and real ghosts, say some, rise from out of the graves at night.

The question is was the ghost Peggy and Denise saw the White Lady of Union Cemetery?

"Be careful what you wish for," Diane Hill likes to tell paranormal enthusiasts who say they want to see ghosts. "You just might get it."

The Story of the White Lady

When I was a newspaper reporter in this area of Suffolk County, I tended to cover stories that were…well, off the beaten path, one might say. As a result, the story of the White Lady was well known to me.

Since I regularly covered the local Sixth Precinct police beat in the Coram-Middle Island area, I would often stop at Union Cemetery and have a look around. I would sit on the hood of my car in the cool of the night and eye the graves. I did this because the Suffolk County Police Department's official blotter records —that I had access to with my reporter's credentials— sometimes mentioned strange sightings at the lonely Middle Island graveyard. I remember one man claimed to have seen a naked woman standing in front of the cemetery. She was unnaturally white. He called the police to investigate. No sign of the woman was found.

In all the years I worked as a reporter in the area, I met only two people who claimed to have actually seen this apparition of a woman appear on the side of the road in front of Union Cemetery. I also met other people who had stories to tell about experiences of which they heard and swore that the people who told them were trustworthy individuals. In all of the cases, the ghost of Union Cemetery was a woman and she was known as the White Lady.

The Sighting

A seasoned ghost investigator, Peggy has captured voices of the dead in the form of EVPs and photographed mystifying manifestations of spirits, including disturbing images on a log in the woods at Sweet Hollow Road in Melville. We discuss these photographs in our 2009 book *Long Island's Most Haunted: A Ghost Hunter's Guide* and exhibit them in a special section on our website. So, Peggy knows the paranormal ropes.

Ghost investigator Peggy Vetrano of Eastern Suffolk Paranormal.

Union Cemetery

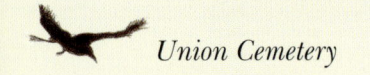

The haunted tree at Union Cemetery. This is where Peggy and Denise saw an apparition on the night of a ghost hunt.

Denise does, too. In fact, Denise photographed one of the rarest images a paranormal investigator can capture — a mist rising out of a grave in broad daylight during warm weather! In addition, like Peggy, she has captured EVPs that could make your hair stand up, including a sort of doomsday EVP inside a car in Union Cemetery. With her recorder on, she posed the following powerful question to the spirits of the graveyard, "Is there a God?"

Later that night, when she reviewed the results of the EVP session, Denise heard a disembodied voice respond, "No!" (*A link to this bone-chilling EVP can be found on ESP's website.*)

As is the case with most other paranormal investigators who belong to ghost research groups across Long Island, Peggy and Denise are detectives of the unknown and, like their colleagues, they are hungry for answers. Ghost investigators are always in search of evidence from beyond the grave. They seek to decipher the meaning of mysteries by unburying pieces of a cryptic puzzle that has baffled humankind since the dawn of civilization. Someday, if Peggy and Denise persist at their work, they may arrive at an answer as to what awaits all of us after death.

Tonight the door between the two worlds opened just long enough for the women to catch a fleeting glimpse of a resident from another place — a place closer than we think, just on the other side of the veil. In the dim crack that opened at Union Cemetery, the investigators were given yet another esoteric clue.

Alertly, Peggy turned to the tree where she had seen the shade of the woman staring vacantly at her from the other side.

"She appeared to have light hair," the intrepid investigator recalled thoughtfully, "but it was so momentary, I'm not sure. I didn't know what I was seeing."

Pointing to Denise, Peggy said suddenly, "She saw it, too. She was looking over my shoulder!"

Peggy seemed happy to remember that she was not alone in this most rare of experiences — that she had validation from another witness who was also an experienced paranormal investigator — since validation is important to ghost investigators in building a case for ghosts at a possible haunted location.

Denise nodded in agreement. She stepped forward to speak to our camera: "Behind the tree tonight I actually saw a flash of light…"

As Denise told her story, she stood at the exact spot where she had witnessed the light and then the subsequent appearance of the apparition. "I told Peggy she should start shooting pictures."

That's when the spirit showed itself.

When asked point blank what they had seen, both women confidently looked dead-on at our video camera and stated they saw "a woman, an apparition." However, the investigators would have to chalk up this amazing visitation to personal experience, for the image of the woman's ghost did not reproduce in their photographs.

Seeing a ghost and photographing a ghost are two different things. In this way, ghost investigators all too often find themselves students in the "School of Hard Knocks and Apparitions." Ghosts don't always show in photographs.

Diane and I once shot video of a ghost moving around a room in Bethpage. Though we could see it in the LCD screen of our video camera, the image did not reproduce to the camera's disk.

Like fishing, there's always a story about the ghost that got away. We all have one. In this case, the one that got away might have been the White Lady of Union Cemetery — or was it? Exactly who the ghostly woman was that Peggy and Denise saw in Union Cemetery remains a mystery. What is known is that a spirit caught in Death's tight grip hovered beside a tree at the back of the mournful graveyard.

Why this unsettled spirit showed itself only to the two ghost investigators and not the others present on the ghost hunt is another mystery. Though there were twelve or more people assembled on this haunting night in the bat-flown graveyard, the spirit decided to reveal itself only to two ghost hunters and not to the other ten. No amount of subsequent provoking, photographing, or wishing for the spirit to materialize could compel the apparition to re-appear for all the rest of us to see.

Was the dead woman's spirit showing itself to the ghost hunters merely to announce her presence in the graveyard in the same way the White Lady appears to drivers on Route 25 in the forlorn mists of the bewitched night?

Did the ghost want Peggy and Denise to know that her poor body is buried in that woeful graveyard and that she is now trapped there as a ghost — or did *she* want to communicate something much more important to Denise and Peggy?

Of course, if she could have communicated, that would have promoted the spirit to the classification of an intelligent entity. Perhaps the spirit ran out of energy before it could tell the investigators what it wanted to say — that is, if the spirit was even aware of their presence.

If the apparition was *residual* — an imprint on the environment — then it was a mere image like a reflection on the surface of black water in a deep dark well and not an intelligent entity at all. In the case of an imprint, the apparition would not have had the ability to communicate just as an image on the surface of a pool of water in a well cannot communicate.

Experiences at Union Cemetery

Denise's and Peggy's mysterious experience with an elusive ghost is not unique at Union Cemetery.

Consider the following paragraph taken with permission from the Long Island Oddities website *(www.lioddities.com)* regarding an experience members had while ghost hunting at Union Cemetery one night long before Denise and Peggy saw the ghost of a woman there.

> "One of our first experiences was with another group. While John (editor) was on the far right side of the cemetery, two women heard his voice distinctly calling out from the complete opposite end of the property. They also claim to have seen what might have been his figure standing in the shadows. While it is possible that in excitement the figure could have been imagined, the two women did not immediately realize the voice was not really from John until they asked over the radio, and there would be little reason to invent the experience."

Union Cemetery

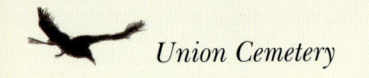

Flashing Lights

Denise and Peggy said they had initially been lured to the area of the tree where they saw the ghost materialize because of a strange light Denise had noticed flashing in the darkness. Upon closer inspection, Denise found that neither an errant flashlight beam nor a passing light cast by a moving car on Route 25 was responsible for the light she saw.

Ghost hunters sometimes refer to these sorts of strange lights as ghost lights. They are occasionally, though rarely, seen by ghost investigators in graveyards and other haunted places.

Some people might also refer to these lights as light orbs or balls of light, though they are of a different character than the typical orbs most often found in photographs. Photographed orbs are usually the result of particles in the air. The light from the camera's flash illuminates the particles and sends their images back to the camera as spherical anomalies. Many people believe orbs may be spirit manifestations. Most ghost investigators dismiss the vast majority of orbs as non-paranormal while reserving others for consideration as true paranormal manifestations. In contrast, ghost lights are commonly seen by the naked eye and are often reported by witnesses at haunted locations.

Denise and Peggy suspected the light Denise saw might have actually been some form of ghostly energy popping in the air. They said they believed whatever energy was creating the light was the same energy that manifested into the apparition they witnessed.

Cold Spot

Denise and Peggy also said that they suspected the spirit remained in the area of the tree after it disappeared. They believed this because "a few minutes later we experienced a cold spot at the exact spot," said Denise.

In fact, later that same night, a mother and daughter ghost hunting team from Manor Park said they had also experienced a cold spot around the same tree where the spirit had been seen. Diane and I recorded the mother and daughter on video sensing this cold spot. In the video, I stuck out my hand towards the tree and reported, "Yes, I feel it, too!" I also felt a distinct difference in the temperature right around the tree.

Paranormal Mist

Laura Leita of Long Island Oddities had a particularly personal experience while she was investigating Union Cemetery one night, which she shares on the group's website at www.lioddities.com.

The most significant event is a strange mist we caught on camera. The weather was chilly and the ground was admittedly damp that night. We split up to cover more ground. During my ramblings I stopped to photograph a particularly interesting tombstone engraved with an anchor. Kneeling in the damp grass with my tripod I took a shot and noticed that it came out rather fuzzy. Intrigued, I looked up from the LCD screen and saw a strange mist just past the tombstone. Fog is a possibility, but usually fog will spread out along the horizon. This was a small 8-10 foot diameter cluster that was about 3 feet in height, give or take a few inches. I took rapid fire still photos as the mist moved closer. It came through the stone toward me, through me, and disappeared somewhere behind me.

Union Cemetery

History of Union Cemetery

Stories of ghosts and paranormal experiences in Union Cemetery have been circulating among Long Island ghost hunters for many years, and possibly among residents of Middle Island for centuries. Though the first recorded grave in the cemetery is that belonging to Daniel Brewster, who died in 1748, historians have suggested people had been buried there previously. The graves are marked by fieldstones without inscriptions. They are located in the northeastern corner of the original one-acre parcel once owned by Middletown Presbyterian Church. The church was located directly across the street from the cemetery. A different church stands there today.

The Connecticut Connection

With respect to ghost lights, apparitions, and moving mists, Long Island's Union Cemetery shares a lot in common with one of the most well-known haunted cemeteries in the Untied States that goes by the same name — Union Cemetery — in Easton, Connecticut. The major similarity between these cemeteries is that they are *both* inhabited by the ghost of a White Lady.

Daniel Brewster's gravesite. He was buried in 1748.

Union Cemetery

Union Cemetery

Easton's Union Cemetery is the place where Ed Warren, the paranormal researcher most famous for his work related to the Amityville Horror case, recorded on video a white ghost floating among graves. As far as we know, the video was never released to the public, but individual frames from the video have appeared in his books.

It all started when Ed Warren became aware through his investigations that ghost lights were appearing at night in rural Union Cemetery, a graveyard located in Easton, a town near Monroe, Connecticut, where Ed lived. He then waited night after night for a week to see the ghost lights appear, believing they were precursors to the materialization of full-bodied apparitions. He wrote that during those nights he had heard the spirits whispering in the graveyard.

One night, after waiting patiently, something amazing happened. Ghost lights began flickering! However, not only did the lights he expected appear, but a ghost came forth as well! It was white and moved among the graves.

"It moved in and out of the graves," said Lorraine Warren, Ed's wife, a psychic and demonologist well-known for her work these days with ghost investigators on the popular television show "Paranormal State."

In a phone conversation, Mrs. Warren told me Ed parked outside the graveyard each night for a week, waiting for the ghosts to appear. She said her husband had been granted permission from the local police to stay on the grounds after dark so he could conduct an investigation.

"It was beautiful," said Mrs. Warren. "He had the tripod set up and his video camera in the car. Then, when the ghost appeared, he went out and put the camera on the tripod and started videotaping."

Ed Warren told the story of his ghost adventure that night at Union Cemetery in *Graveyard*, a book he and Lorraine co-authored in 1992. He said the ghost that appeared to him was a woman about thirty years old. Around her were other spirits that seemed to be arguing with her.

Though Ed Warren did show the amazing video to fellow members of the New England Society for Psychic Research, sadly, he never released it to the public. He died in August 2006 at age 79. He had suffered a stroke about five years earlier and reportedly never fully regained his speech.

In some ways, Diane and I consider ourselves students of the Warrens' work. This led us to visit Union Cemetery in Easton, Connecticut, several times to see for ourselves what Ed Warren had seen at the graveyard.

Diane and I lingered in the area for a couple of days during one visit to Connecticut, interviewing people and receiving personal tours of the graveyard and the local area. We also received a tour of another graveyard, Stepney Cemetery, in nearby Monroe, where Ed Warren was laid to rest. It was at Stepney Cemetery where a person we interviewed saw two ghostly priests walking and where the Lady in White is known to sometimes appear. The Lady is often seen walking the road between Easton and Monroe.

"She travels back and forth," we were told by a local man, who claims to have seen with his own two eyes the mysterious White Lady walking the road.

Opposite: Union Cemetery in Easton, Connecticut is where Ed Warren, the paranormal researcher of the Amityville Horror case, videotaped a white ghost.

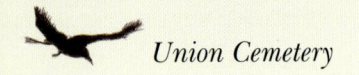

Voices in the Wind

I must admit, I go to Union Cemetery often, mostly to try to understand the puzzle of the White Lady.

I live in Rocky Point, a nearby hamlet, so it's not a big journey for me to drive seven miles south on Rocky Point Road, into Middle Island, and then swing west on Route 25 and drive a mile to the cemetery. When I'm alone at Union, I usually sit on a bench installed by an Eagle Scout not far from the haunted tree and do a little writing or reading. It's a great quiet spot to be left alone.

While Seaview Cemetery, located adjacent to the Mt. Sinai Congregational Church on North Country Road in Mt. Sinai, is my favorite local place to just walk and empty my head or write in a black and white marble notebook, it is not a haunted place and this fact is detraction from its appeal to me. In fact, I find Seaview Cemetery to be paranormally inactive.

Ironically, Seaview is the cemetery some ghost hunters claim Devil's Gate or Satan's Trails originate. Supposedly, the place is haunted. Long Island Oddities debunked these myths about the location many years ago, but like bad wine, the tiresome legends continue to ferment. To learn more about this cemetery, visit our website and go to the Investigations page.

So when I'm in the mood to relax while also keeping an eye out for ghosts, I go to Union Cemetery in nearby Middle Island because it offers the best of both worlds, as voices do carry in the wind at Union Cemetery. In this way, it is also very similar to Union Cemetery in Easton, Connecticut, where Ed Warren experienced the whispering of spirits. Diane and I have also heard whispers in the wind there.

I am not much of an EVP person because I find most EVPs I record sound identical to plain electronic junk, so I don't bother to do much recording in graveyards. Nor does Diane do much EVP work. However, I must say I have heard some excellent first-class EVPs recorded by some top-notch Long Island ghost investigators, such as Peggy and Denise, Mike Salvia, Brigid Goode, and Chris Griffith, but when it comes to my own, the EVPs sound like a jacket zipper being pulled up and I don't trust them enough to call them voices of the dead.

This is not to say I haven't heard spirits talk.

To the contrary, the most frightening and loudest scream I ever heard was from a ghost. It lasted many seconds and actually had a physical dimension to it — a wind that rushed into my face and made me close my eyes. It felt like fingers going around my head. The feeling was very close to that of putting your face close to a blasting guitar amplifier.

The laughing black birds of Union Cemetery. *Drawing by Karen Isaksen.*

Union Cemetery

Often, at random locations, I hear voices of spirits saying things that have no relevance to me at the moment, or even thereafter, such as "Doug," "thank you," or "no." Usually, they're said at moments when I am not doing anything or even thinking anything that deserves a "thank you" or a "no" — and I have no idea who "Doug" is!

At any rate, one spring day, while I was at Union Cemetery by myself, a voice floated to me in the wind. I wasn't sure what the voice was saying, but it grabbed my attention a few times. It was a male voice.

The mid-April Monday was warm and sunny. I was comfortable wearing only a T-shirt and a sweater. Of course, I had our Sony DSC F828 digital camera, which we lovingly refer to as "The Dark Angel," strapped to my neck, clicking off photos as I slowly wandered the grounds, letting my head empty of compressed thoughts and daily worries.

The distinct feeling of a set of eyes watching me suddenly commanded my attention. I was strolling around, reading the inscriptions and looking for signs of the paranormal, when an

An orb appears in the afternoon sunlight in front of the haunted tree at Union Cemetery.   Is it dust or some kind of spiritual manifestation?

unsettling feeling overtook me, followed by a sickly feeling that entered my chest.

I was familiar with this sickly feeling. It's the feeling both Diane and I get when the spirits are nearby. I learned to recognize this feeling early on in my development as a ghost investigator, but on this day I saw nothing out of the ordinary as I looked around, scrutinizing the green terrain. I was the only person in the entire cemetery.

I quickly turned around and snapped off a photograph with The Dark Angel.

Immediately afterwards I looked at the LCD screen on the back of the camera and saw I had captured something — a shadow of something in front of a grave. Moreover, a white mist seemed to be hovering before the grave or possibly rising from it. *(It can be viewed by visiting our website.)*

Later at home, in our studio, I would make out a dark shadowy figure lurching over the grave. My intense scrutiny of the photo led me to believe the shadow was that of a spirit looking back at me. The shadow person appeared to be wearing a large black hat. The mist seemed to be hovering before the top of the stone.

At the moment I took the photo in the cemetery, however, I was not sure what I had photographed because I could not see its details on the camera's small LCD screen, so I continued walking with the camera readied in my hand. I walked with my eyes closed so I could hear any sounds more distinctly.

"Who are you?" I asked.

Certainly, if anybody had seen me walking like Dr. Frankenstein with my eyes closed, they would have immediately went the opposite way, thinking I was nuts. However, since nobody was there, I was free to experiment any way I wished.

"Who are you?" I asked again.

A voice floated back to me in the light breeze. "Ready," it said distinctly.

I had no idea what this meant and I opened my eyes and looked around. I realized then that I was standing in front of the haunted tree where Peggy and Denise had seen the apparition of a woman in a long dress. I snapped a photo of the tree and, in it, I could immediately see I had captured a white orb floating before its trunk.

I am not a believer that orbs are paranormal manifestations, but the issue does blur sometimes. It seems that many times when paranormal manifestations, such as mists, light rods, or apparitions, do appear in photos, orbs are also present. Many people have reported to us that they photographed orbs at haunted locations just seconds before or after being touched, or just seconds before or after hearing a disembodied voice.

Since it has long been our belief that orbs, the most common form of which are translucent spherical anomalies in photographs, are the result of dust, pollen, bugs, rain drops, snow flakes, animal dander, or some other material in the air, I didn't give much credence to the orb I saw floating in front of the haunted tree. However, I will admit I was surprised by the orbs' appearance following the voice in the wind I had heard only a seconds before — and only a half a minute after I also photographed a shadow lurching above a gravestone and mist floating before it.

Things seemed to snap together and fit at that moment in time. It appeared that the graveyard was coming alive with paranormal activity.

I had seen this happen on a number of other occasions. It's like the music of a dysfunctional symphony that clangs and clashes together at the increasing pace of one's own fast beating heart. All the strings are out of tune, the bass drum is out of time, and the music is a strange cacophony of the unfamiliar and bizarre. At these moments it's my job to hear the symphony and try to understand its chaotic themes.

A Bird's Call

"Lead me to you," I demanded. "Bring me to your grave and appear to me so I can photograph you and show the world that there is another side."

I began walking again. Just then a crow squawked loudly behind me.

I immediately turned back. It was the only crow squawk I had heard since I had arrived in the graveyard, and since I had nothing else to work on, I followed the direction of the bird's cry.

"I'm waiting for another instruction," I said to the air, as I continued walking west, towards the newer part of the cemetery.

I was now on the narrow cemetery road that runs beside a chain link fence separating the cemetery from a golf course. I looked up and saw the crow that had made the squawk flap into the air from a tree and fly to another tree in a patch of woods separating

These woods divide parts of Union Cemetery. This is where the whispering spirits led Joseph Flammer one April day, but what's here besides the remains of an old farmhouse? Could it be that the property is haunted not by ghosts from the graves, but by the former landowners?

Union Cemetery

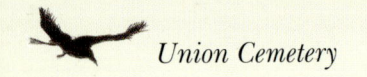

the main portion of the cemetery from another smaller section at the far western side of the property. The bird cawed again. I picked up my pace to get to the area of woods to accommodate the flow of information the bird was feeding me — or at least I assumed it was feeding me.

The woods contain mounds of dirt and vegetation debris. I walked up the mounds and inspected everything. I found bricks and possibly a chimney from a house that must have once been on the land many years ago. The original owner of the property was Stephen Swezey. He had owned a large farm on the land and sold some of the property to his son, James, who sold it to his son, Robert, and so on. Many members of that early family are now buried in Union Cemetery.

Just then, I heard a whispering voice in the wind, but I couldn't tell what it was saying because it was too faint.

"Why don't you show yourself to me?" I asked the woods. "Come out and show yourself."

"All gone," the voice responded. This time it was a woman's whisper, not a man's.

I looked around at the mounds, the trees, and a sort of path that ran between the woods. Curiously, I wondered why I was standing in the woods of a graveyard. Why would the spirits want me here? Aren't the dead in the graveyard proper?

Just then the crow squawked and flew off towards the area I had just come from. Suddenly, it squawked many times. The squawking sounded like laughter. I thought I heard whispering follow behind it.

"Are you playing with me?" I asked the spirits.

There was no response. There was only the empty feeling of being alone in a haunted graveyard.

The author Joe Flammer saw a crow cawing over graves. Was it a sign of some kind? Drawing by Karen Isaksen.

I suddenly understood the feelings Ed Warren felt at Union Cemetery in Easton, Connecticut, when he heard whispers carried to him on the breeze. I marveled at the many similarities between the two cemeteries. I wondered if the woman's voice I heard saying, "All gone," was the voice of the spirit that Peggy and Denise had seen in the light of the camera's flash that very fateful night. Was she the ghost known as the White Lady?

6

Pine Hollow Cemetery
Oyster Bay

Location: Off Route 106 in Oyster Bay

Description: Pine Hollow is a small historic cemetery, only several acres big with perhaps two hundred graves.

How to get there: This cemetery is located on a small street, just south of the Mill-Max building off the west side of Pine Hollow Road (the local name for Route 106) in Oyster Bay. Route 106 can be reached by the Long Island Expressway at Exit 41 North. From the LIE go north and stay to the right as Route 106 and Route 107 fork away from each other with 106 quickly veering to the right. The cemetery is located across the street from a strip mall in which a CVS and a Dunkin Donuts are located.

Sign at the entrance to Pine Hollow Cemetery.

Pine Hollow Cemetery

This view of a haunted hill in Pine Hollow Cemetery was taken in early spring.   This is the area where the grim ghost in the flowing black cape appears.

A Restless Place of the Dead

The grim ghost in the flowing black cape has been seen again, but this time his head is missing!

Ghostly experiences are common in Pine Hollow Cemetery in Oyster Bay. Photographs of paranormal mists, ghostly orbs, and streaking light anomalies have launched this ill-fitting place to the top of the list of Long Island's most haunted graveyards, but there is one experience beyond all others that still haunts ghost investigators who visit this spirit-filled graveyard — photographing the elusive ghost that appears on the haunted hill.

Sightings of full-bodied apparitions have been reported on or around the haunted hill in Pine Hollow Cemetery. The descriptions of these commanding spirits are strikingly similar, as witnesses have reported the sudden appearance of a ghostly man in dark clothing. The foreboding entity scowls, but does not speak. He flashes a black cape similar to those worn by Union soldiers during the Civil War and vanishes before anyone can photograph him.

Almost every ghost hunter we speak with who has visited Pine Hollow has a story to tell about their supernatural experiences in this restless place of the dead. The unsettling stories include being touched, hearing strange growls, and seeing unusual shadows and fleeting balls of light. Many people feel they are followed or watched as they walk the grounds.

Stories of paranormal activity at this mournful location are too many to list, but some of the notable ones include a pair of psychics who claimed their investigation of this historic graveyard was interrupted by *unseen soldiers on horseback* that escorted them off the property.

Other investigators report experiencing paranormal phenomena when they return home from this estranged place — one woman said she was awakened by dancing lights in her bedroom following her first ghost hunt at Pine Hollow!

Pine Hollow's History

Pine Hollow was once considered a "negro" cemetery. It's the final resting place of seven brave African Americans who joined the Union Army to fight in the Civil War, including David Carll, who was shot through the lung while fighting with the colored infantry during a fierce battle against the Confederates. He survived the wound and returned home to Oyster Bay.

David Carll's family plot is on the small hill where most of the reported ghostly activity takes place.

A paranormal mist forms over the graves at Pine Hollow Cemetery.

Pine Hollow Cemetery

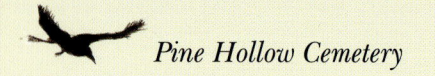

While members of the Carll family may not be the spirits haunting the cemetery, the hill and the area around the hill is nonetheless where apparitions have been seen in broad daylight and where the most haunting photographs have been taken.

The Little Boy and the Flag

Chris Griffith is an experienced paranormal investigator from Lake Ronkonkoma. Tonight he brought his fifteen-year-old niece, Angelica Miceli, to Pine Hollow Cemetery because she was anxious to ghost hunt with him in this legendary graveyard.

Chris and Angelica arrived just as the fiery red summer sun sank behind the lush green trees in the woods on the hills rising up behind Pine Hollow. Chris had been to this haunted graveyard before, so he was familiar with the rugged terrain. He wanted his niece to see the layout of the place before darkness fell.

Angelica was no stranger to graveyards or ghost hunts. She had accompanied her Uncle Chris, a member of the ghost hunting group The Paranormal Investigators, on a visit to Potter's Field in Yaphank. It was there that she encountered a shadow person. Spirits seem to be drawn to Angelica.

Whenever Chris visits Pine Hollow, he feels as if he is being watched by unseen entities. "I'm not frightened, but I often get chills and the hair on the back of my neck stands up," Chris told us. This is a common experience among ghost hunters at this old burying ground.

Chris and Angelica strolled beneath the soaring trees in the fading daylight. They began photographing the desolate graveyard as night crept in and surrounded them.

They settled on the sloping haunted hill behind the Carll family plot as the cicadas serenaded them on this balmy sum-

A mist forms near David Carll's grave.

Pine Hollow Cemetery

mer night. The cemetery was still and peaceful. The nearly full moon cast long shadows over the graves in this final resting place of the dead.

"Look at that flag, Uncle Chris!" Angelica exclaimed, yanking on his shirtsleeve and pointing to a grave on the slope before them. "The flag on that grave is moving, but there's no wind! The leaves aren't moving at all!"

Chris raised an eyebrow and, looking up at the trees, reasoned, "Maybe there's a slight breeze we can't feel."

Above: A ghostly boy tugs on the flag in front of David Carll's grave. *Courtesy of Chris Griffith.*

Left: Ghost investigator Chris Griffith of The Paranormal Investigators and his niece Angelica. *Courtesy of Michele Snow.*

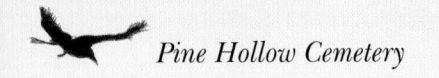

"But a breeze would wave the flag side-to-side," Angelica countered. "That flag is moving up and down like someone is tugging on it!"

Chris studied the flag. "You're right!" he said, and grabbed his camera and began shooting.

The pair reviewed the photographs Chris had just taken on the camera's LCD screen. They were stunned at what they saw — the ghostly shape of a young boy was leaning over the gravestone and tugging on the red, white, and blue American flag attached to a small rod bearing the Civil War veteran's emblem. All the profound feelings of the paranormal Chris had ever experienced — chills, hair standing up on the back of his neck, the sound of his breathing, and the loud beating of his heart in his ears — rushed at him now.

Then the flag fell still. Angelica called out, "David, can you move the flag again?"

Chris looked at his niece in amazement and asked, "How do you know his name is David?"

"I read it on the headstone earlier," she answered with grin.

It was the grave of David Carll, Civil War veteran and patriarch of the Carll family. To their amazement, the flag suddenly moved up and down again as they watched. Chris and Angelica knew they were witnessing a paranormal event — an occurrence like this is rare even for ghost hunters.

A moment later the flag fell once more.

"We mean you no harm or disrespect," Angelica called out to the young spirit.

The flag didn't move again. The pair waited awhile longer, but young David seemed to be done playing for the evening.

As Chris and Angelica made their way down the haunted hill, Chris paused and said a silent thanks to David Carll for giving Angelica a clear sign of his presence and making her first visit to Pine Hollow Cemetery a memorable one.

The Ghost with No Head

Mark Koenigsmann from Massapequa Park is a retired emergency medical technician (EMT) paramedic. He's responded to hundreds of medical emergencies and is familiar with the human body and the fragility of life. Perhaps that's why he became a paranormal enthusiast and, as an avid Civil War buff and researcher, he is drawn to Pine Hollow Cemetery, where there are seven Civil War veterans buried.

Typically, Mark investigates Pine Hollow Cemetery during daylight hours with his thirteen-year-old son Dave. However, one bright sunny afternoon, Mark visited Pine Hollow alone and, as he walked through the graveyard, he felt as though he was being watched. He got a strange tingling sensation.

"The hackles on the back of my neck were standing on edge," he recalled.

Mark walked up the wide grassy path and turned left just before the haunted hill, making his way toward the oldest section of the cemetery. As he entered this area, he felt "out of sorts."

"I had a really strong feeling of being watched. At the same time I caught a black or dark blue figure to my left, just in the periphery of my vision. I turned to look, but nothing was there."

Mark took a couple of steps. The feeling only intensified.

"I spotted the figure again out of the corner of my eye. It seemed to be about six feet tall and sturdily built, but it had no head. The figure wore a jacket with a sort of cape. It was flowing. The image lasted only seconds and then it was gone. I was not startled and, remarkably, not at all frightened."

Mark later researched Civil War uniforms and found the coat the apparition wore was similar to the Union Army "greatcoat."

Mark continued photographing, hoping the spirit would return so he could capture it in photographs. He was disappointed that the apparition had faded away so quickly.

Pine Hollow Cemetery

About that time, the cemetery's groundskeeper showed up. He and Mark spoke about the storied history of the old graveyard, but unfortunately, all the books containing the early history of the cemetery had been lost in a fire. The only records left are those from the last twenty-six years, according to the groundskeeper.

During his conversation with the groundskeeper, Mark noticed a black cat suddenly appear on the haunted hill.

"It took two or three steps and sat watching us," he said. "A few minutes later, it just disappeared!"

Mark explained he would have seen it if it ran into the woods, but it seems the cat just vanished.

The Mystery of the Flying Black Ball

Two days after seeing the headless ghost, Mark returned to the haunted cemetery with his son Dave. They brought along divining rods and a camera. Father and son spoke to the spirits as they used the divining rods and took pictures. Dave was hoping to see a ghost. He knew this place had a reputation for being haunted.

This light anomaly appeared near the haunted hill in Pine Hollow Cemetery. *Courtesy of Mark Koenigsmann.*

Pine Hollow Cemetery

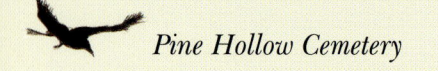

The duo was preparing to leave after thoroughly exploring and photographing the graveyard when Dave asked his dad, "Why do you get all the good pictures and see the good stuff?"

"Open up and it will come to you, too," Mark assured his son.

Mark then turned to study a set of Civil War soldiers' graves on the left side of the haunted hill.

Suddenly, Dave loudly exclaimed, "Wow! Did you see that?"

Startled, Mark's attention shot back to his son.

"A black ball flew over David Carll's gravestone and disappeared!" Dave's voice crackled with excitement. "Did you see it?"

"No, I didn't," his dad answered.

Mark's eyes scanned the lonely haunted hill just beyond David Carll's grave. He felt the familiar tingle of the paranormal shoot through his body as his adrenalin surged. Somewhere out there, beyond his vision, in an unknown dimension a spirit prowled, calling out for attention.

Dave smiled broadly. He wasn't upset or afraid. He was thrilled to finally experience something paranormal for himself!

A paranormal mist moves through Pine Hollow Cemetery. The mist disappears only to appear in a different part of the graveyard a moment later.

Mark quickly turned his camera toward David Carll's grave and began snapping photographs, but the elusive black ball did not appear again.

However, it seems that the spirits had heard Dave's request. They not only benevolently granted his wish, but he witnessed something very few people see — Dave saw an orb in motion!

Shall We Be Seated?

It seems the spirits of Pine Hollow Cemetery have no qualms about letting ghost hunters know when they've overstayed their welcome. The following is a true account of a woman, Kerry Abelow from Amityville, who sat on a gravestone during an investigation, unwittingly irritating the spirits.

We were running late as we pulled into the busy CVS parking lot on Route 106. A small group of people with cameras and voice recorders waved to us as I maneuvered my black SUV into a parking space. Joe, psychic John Altieri, and I jumped out of the truck with our equipment and joined our fellow paranormal investigators for a night of good old-fashioned ghost hunting at one of our favorite haunts, Pine Hollow Cemetery.

The hour was approaching 9 o'clock on this summer evening. We trooped across Route 106 in the fading blue light of dusk and gathered in the graveyard's small dirt parking lot. The light of a silvery full moon washed over the white wooden arch at the cemetery's entrance where bold black letters announced "Pine Hollow Cemetery, Established 1884."

We stood in a circle under the archway. In the glittering moonlight, we held hands. I recited our familiar entreaty assuring the spirits we were there not to disturb their peace or harm them, but to try and gather evidence of what, if anything, lies beyond the grave. I asked the dead to reveal themselves to our cameras and speak into our voice recorders.

With that said, we embarked on our hunt. The more seasoned ghost hunters scattered throughout the cemetery and began taking photographs and attempting to do EVP sessions while first-time ghost hunters trailed behind veterans asking questions and trying to absorb all they could. The crickets were so loud on this balmy Long Island summer night it was impossible to capture any clear EVPs.

Psychics John Altieri of North Babylon and Barbara Loiko of Farmingdale were first-time visitors to Pine Hollow Cemetery. Upon entering the graveyard, they both felt pulled to an area on the left side of the haunted hill.

The fragrance of talcum powder mixed with the odor of saddle oil permeated the air and drew the psychics away from the rest of us into a darker, deeper area of the cemetery. All the while Altieri and Loiko felt like they were being followed by invisible entities on horseback.

Even though they could see the rest of the group from the remote area where they stood, both psychics said that they felt oddly separated from us.

"I felt as though I had crossed over into another time... another era," Loiko stated.

After about ten minutes, the fragrance dissipated and the strange feelings evaporated into the recesses of the mysterious graveyard.

Joe was standing on the haunted hill. He was facing forward overlooking the cemetery with the woods behind him. As he stood there, he gradually felt his chest begin to tighten and a familiar sickly feeling overtook him. The nerve-endings in his body were on high alert. In his experience, this meant only one thing — spirits were present.

Pine Hollow Cemetery

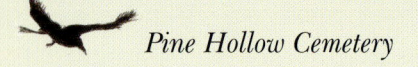

"I was being watched and followed by someone or something…I knew instinctively it was behind me lurking in the woods. I turned around, but there was nothing I could see. I snapped off two photographs in quick succession and then my camera died. I had just charged the battery that morning so that should not have happened. I pulled out my video camera, which I had fully charged that same day, and found it was dead, too. This was a most unusual experience. At that point I knew the ghost drifting among the trees was sending me a clear message. It did not want me to photograph it."

Right about this time, Brigid Goode, a member of The Paranormal Investigators, was standing on the grassy slope of the haunted hill. She was photographing with her deep infrared camera and captured an image of what many of us believe is the spirit of a black man standing behind Joe. Why did the spirit allow Brigid to photograph him and not Joe? It seems spirits, just like humans, have a mind and a will all of their own.

This Way Out

Meanwhile, psychics Altieri and Loiko had rejoined the group in the main part of the cemetery, but not for long. The spirits lured them up the haunted hill to the edge of the woods that bordered the graveyard.

"I heard heavy, thumping footsteps and felt an immediate presence," recalled Altieri. "A dark shadow moved through the woods and the name 'David' kept coming to mind."

Psychics John Altieri and Barbara Loiko sense spirits in the woods on Sweet Hollow Road. Months later, the two would be escorted out of Pine Hollow Cemetery by unseen spirits on horseback.

Pine Hollow Cemetery

This haunted hill is where the elusive grim ghost has been seen, but never photographed.

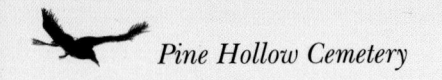

It was at this point that several of us sat down on the haunted hill to observe and meditate.

I was sitting on the crest of the hill facing the entrance when first-time ghost hunter, Kerry Abelow, made a seat for herself on top of a granite headstone located near the bottom of the haunted hill. In doing so, she inadvertently caused a rock that had been placed atop the headstone by a visitor to be knocked to the ground.

Though Kerry apologized to the spirits of the cemetery for appearing disrespectful, explaining that her back hurt and she could not sit on the ground, those of us seated on the hill above her did not hear her apology. We grew uneasy when she lowered herself onto the headstone because we did not want to anger the spirits, especially in this graveyard where people have heard threatening growls in the night and glimpsed malevolent ghosts in daylight.

Unexpectedly, and without a word, the two psychics came marching down the hill and headed directly to the white archway at the entrance of the cemetery. They looked straight ahead and walked stiffly side-by-side in step with each other. "Just like soldiers," I thought to myself as I watched them pass under the arched sign and exit the cemetery.

Later, both Altieri and Loiko said they felt compelled by the spirits to get out of the cemetery at once. The pair sensed they were being escorted out by soldiers on horseback.

"I could smell the leather saddle," Altieri said.

"I could almost feel the tip of a boot touching my shoulder as I walked down the hill," added Loiko.

Even though the woman who sat on the headstone meant no disrespect, the psychics felt the spirits were angered by her actions. Once they crossed into the cemetery's parking lot, Altieri and Loiko noticed the pungent scent of leather was replaced by the sweet smell of fresh flowers. The psychics agreed it was a "thank you" from the spirits for honoring the wishes of the graveyard's dead and leaving the cemetery.

The rest of our ghost hunting party decided we wouldn't wait for a ghostly escort. We quickly gathered our equipment and followed Altieri and Loiko out of the spooky graveyard.

Best Not to Anger the Spirits

However, the miffed spirits of Pine Hollow were not about to let this matter die so easily. At 3 a.m., Abelow witnessed paranormal phenomena inside her own bedroom.

> "I was lying there wide awake, but with my eyes closed. I guess I was keyed up because I was excited about having gone on my first official ghost hunt. The fan was on so there was white noise. I heard 'pssssst' and a second later 'pssssst' again. I opened my eyes and looked up at the clock radio that was on a high shelf across the room. I could see the numbers fine, but it was doing a light show. It was flashing like disco lights."

Startled, Abelow sat up. She grabbed a book off her nightstand and read a page to prove she was actually awake.

When she realized she wasn't dreaming, she told whatever was in the room to go away and leave her alone. Then, she lay back down, closed her eyes, and willed herself to fall asleep.

Abelow has not seen the disco show again. Were the dancing lights a direct consequence of her sitting on top of the headstone in the spirited graveyard that night?

Conclusion

The ghosts of Pine Hollow Cemetery are trying to communicate. What is their message? Who will be the first person to photograph the mysterious spirit of the black-caped man on the haunted hill? Maybe it will be you!

7

Sagtikos Manor

West Bay Shore

Location: North side of Montauk Highway (Route 27A), West Bay Shore.

Description: A small family cemetery in a treed area located behind an historic house called Sagtikos Manor. The land was purchased from Native American's who called the land they sold "the Hissing Snake." Today the mansion is a museum.

How to get there: Take Robert Moses Causeway South to Exit RM 2E (Rt. 27A) Bay Shore. Turn right onto Rt. 27A and continue east approximate half mile. Entrance to Sagtikos Manor will be on the left.

The rear of Sagtikos Manor faces the graveyard located across the property.

Sagtikos Manor

This is the Gardiner-Thompson Family Graveyard at Sagtikos Manor.

The Gardiner-Thompson Family Cemetery

One thing is for sure — if ever there was a house on Long Island obviously haunted, it's Sagtikos Manor on Montauk Highway in West Bay Shore.

While the building itself, now a museum, is reputed to be haunted — and as you will see, there is reason for us to believe it is — it's the tiny graveyard behind the house that should capture the interest of ghost hunters.

The country landscape unabashedly abounds with paranormal energy. Effects of the supernatural in this cemetery can be sensed, felt, seen, photographed, and even captured on audio recorders.

The Hissing Snake

The exact meaning of the Secatogue Indian word "Sagtikos" is in dispute.

An old-timer from Bay Shore whom I interviewed in the 1970s told me the land, now occupied by Sagtikos Parkway, a state road

Sagtikos Manor as seen from Montauk Highway.

Sagtikos Manor

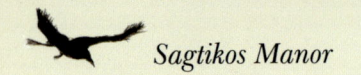

due north of the Manor, was at one time the only place in the world where a tiny white snake could be found. He said Sagtikos means "white snake."

However, the museum staff who give tours of the old house and its remaining ten acres say "Sagtikos" is an old Indian word for "hissing snake."

Nobody is sure why back in the late 1600s Native Americans called the original 1,207 acres of Sagtikos Manor "the hissing snake." It might have been because on a map the original property was shaped like a snake.

Certainly the image of a hissing snake ready to strike is not comforting. What dark secrets did the Indians know about this property that we don't?

Haunted Graveyard

"There's no mistaking I saw a ghost!" insisted Lisa Michaels of Islip. "There's no mistaking. She just vanished!"

The ghost of a young lady from the colonial period, in a long gray dress, dark shawl, and a white colonial cap, appeared to Michaels and her sister on a cold, gray blustery day in the 1980s when brown, gold, and red leaves blew in the wind like lost memories.

The sisters had come to the Manor that overcast autumn day to take a tour of the sleepy mansion and the stark grounds, but tours were not offered. The museum was closed. The property was deserted, so they took a short walk to the small and mysterious graveyard behind the mansion.

View of the back of the mansion from outside the cemetery.

View of small family graveyard behind Sagtikos Manor.

Sagtikos Manor

The old dark graves inside the Gothic cemetery are surrounded by a rusted, black, wrought iron fence. The great gate groaned from lack of use when the sisters pushed it forward and stepped inside into another time period.

"Nobody was there," recalled Michaels.

For the benefit of our video camera, she pointed at the white mansion as she stood in the field of tall trees behind the building.

"We banged on the windows and the doors, hoping somebody would be there, but no one was," she said. "The mansion was closed, so we figured we'd walk the grounds and visit the cemetery on the property."

Michaels said she and her sister were standing inside the small cemetery reading the names on the old brown and gray headstones when the ghost of a young woman suddenly appeared and walked past the cemetery.

"She wore a shawl and a colonial styled hat and smiled at us. Then, she nodded her head to us in greeting," recalled Michaels. "Not five seconds later she just vanished! There was no place for her to hide. Even if she could, why would she hide?"

The sisters were shocked. "We looked at each other and said, 'Let's get out of here!' We hopped in the car and took off!"

Michaels later returned to the Manor for the tour. She told the people who worked there what she saw.

"'Oh, that would be Mary Gardiner,' they said. They told me other people had seen her, too. They told me she is buried in this cemetery."

Michaels entered the cemetery through the heavy iron gate as we followed with our video camera.

"I haven't seen any ghosts before or afterwards," she said. "I have a theory that the reason why Mary Gardiner appeared to us was because she was lonely. She missed the company of other young women who she could talk with and exchange ideas."

Lisa Michaels points to the place where she saw the ghost of a young woman dressed in colonial clothing. She was told by the museum staff that she saw the ghost of Mary Gardiner, who is buried in the cemetery. Notice the light anomaly near Lisa's knee: is it a light flare or yet another sign from the spirits?

Sagtikos Manor

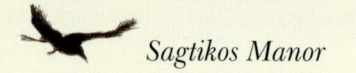

Moving Mists

In these photographs, you can see a mist moving across the graveyard. This mist was visible to the naked eye. I asked Diane to freeze in place (below) so I could photograph it. A moment later, it sat over a grave.

Sagtikos Manor

Diane Hill watches as a paranormal mist that moved across the graveyard at Sagtikos Manor settles on an old grave.

115

Sagtikos Manor

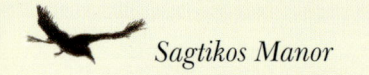

Spirits Moving in the Night

Left: Diane communes with the spirits as psychic John Altieri observes and takes photographs. Earlier, while alone in the cemetery, Diane felt a child's hand take hold of hers. At the same time her voice recorder captured the sounds of a creaking box — like the lid of a coffin either opening or closing — but the sounds and the touch of the spirit's hand would only come to her when she was alone. If another person entered the cemetery that night, the noises immediately stopped and the spirits withdrew.

Above: Notice the orb over the sarcophagus beside psychic John Altieri. Is this the same orb that was photographed next to two local ghost hunters Joe met outside the cemetery later that night (see left)?

Sagtikos Manor

A spirit in the night dances as a mist in the center of the photo. This mist drifted in the air above the courtyard at Sagtikots Manor.

Sagtikos Manor

Do you see figures in the mist? A cold air drifted by as this paranormal mist passed through the courtyard at Sagtikos Manor. Though many more photographs were taken on this night, only two contained the mist. It hovered above us for a brief period of about ten seconds, during which time a cold air could be felt and sounds of distant whispers filled the night.

A Tour of the Manor

The Sagtikos Manor Historical Society offers tours of the Manor during limited hours on certain days of the week during the warmer seasons. They also hold special events year-round including a harvest season festival.

Diane and I have visited the Manor many times after sunset. We have listened to the rustling wind in the big trees in the open space of the yard near the cemetery in the back of the house. We have taken photos and talked to the spirits.

One early Sunday afternoon in July Diane and I took the official historical society tour of the Manor. It lasted about an hour and cost $7.00 each. Photography is not allowed inside the house "because of security concerns," said our tour guide.

Admittedly, Diane and I were disappointed with the no photography rule. We have been to many museums, such as Raynham Hall in Oyster Bay, where photography is freely permitted and even encouraged. It makes the tour experience much more fun and personal. Let's face it, even non-ghost hunters enjoy the possibility of capturing ghostly images in photographs taken at historical sites. That's part of the allure of digging into history.

The tour guides referred to themselves as "docents." They were dressed in clothing that represented the colonial and Edwardian historical periods. Additions were made to the house during these periods. One of the docents told us she bought her colonial costume on eBay.

We had eight different guides during our tour of the house, each one knowledgeable about the particular part of the Manor of which they spoke. Thus, the guides passed visitors on to each other in a chain that starts with the newest addition to the building, the music room in the east wing. Then tourists are passed to the second oldest period of the Manor, built in the 1700s and 1800s. From there tourists are sent to the original four rooms of the oldest part of the house, dating back to the late 1690s. The tour ends in the west wing's gift shop where trinkets can be purchased.

The only other person with us when we took the tour was a woman from Minnesota. She wanted to buy a book about the Manor's history at the gift shop, but the gift shop doesn't sell such history books. The docent suggested the woman go online and find the written history there.

The oldest part of the house, which included the kitchen with a big fireplace, a parlor, and two small bedrooms on the first floor, are simply furnished. Everything is fixed up to look like it would have appeared in the old days.

The house was built in 1697 by the Van Cortlandt family, probably to serve as a hunting lodge. The original property of 1,207 acres extended in a long narrow strip of land a mile wide, from the Great South Bay eight miles straight north.

George Washington Slept Here

Of course, there is some rich history to the Manor, with the most historic event taking place when George Washington stayed for one night in 1790 during his famous five-day tour of Long Island. We saw the bedroom where he stayed. There was not much more to it than a bed. We were not permitted in the room. We had to stand in the doorway and gape.

We also saw where a musket ball was shot by a British soldier at the owner of the house during the American Revolution. According to the story we were told, the shot was fired at the owner of the house when he stopped on the second floor landing with a lantern to gaze out the window at the Great South Bay at dusk. English soldiers, who were encamped on the grounds, thought he was signaling some kind of attack on their forces. One of the soldiers took a shot to stop him. The man was not hurt. The musket ball lodged in the wall beside the staircase leading to the attic.

Probably the most interesting aspect of the tour was seeing how our ancestors performed mundane tasks. They used clever tools to toast bread and to retrieve hot pots from over burning fires in the kitchen fireplace.

Mostly what I walked away with from the Manor was an impression of how rich families who owned the mansion and land enjoyed privilege and status. We learned that some former owners of the Manor had slaves. Other owners, in later years, had up to seven paid servants. It is presumed the slaves were buried near the family graveyard located only a short walk from the house, but there are no grave markers.

We were not permitted to view the cellar or the attic, so we don't know what kind of dark mysteries might lurk there. Diane and I once investigated the remains of a mansion in Patchogue that had a slave pen in the cellar. It was said that the ghostly screams of the tortured slaves could be heard from that pen long after the building was abandoned.

One of the docents told us a Native American girl was also buried on the Manor's property. The guide said a plaque dedicated to the young Indian girl was affixed to the fence that surrounds the small family cemetery behind the house, but that it fell off a few years ago and has since been stolen.

Diane and I looked gravely at each other when we heard that the Indian girl's plaque was stolen because we have heard many stories of people taking things related to the dead and later paying dire consequences for it.

For example, we learned of a tragic event associated with a teenager stealing a gravestone from a cemetery at night in Adams, Tennessee, where we spent four days investigating the Bell Witch Ghost that killed John Bell in 1820. It's the only documented case of an entity killing a human in the United States. We learned the teenager had stolen the stone from John Bell's grave on the former Bell farm in the 1950s. He was killed in a car crash that very night. Police found the gravestone in the trunk of his car. The dead boy's mother returned the stone to John Bell's gravesite.

The Residents of the Manor

There were two main families that occupied the Manor since it was built in 1697: the Thompsons and the Gardiners (of the Gardiners Island lineage). They were cousins. They intermarried twice to keep the Manor inside the families, we were told.

When things got tough, some of the owners sold off the property until it dwindled down to just ten acres. Then, in 2002, the last "Lord of the Manor," Robert David Lion Gardiner, sold the house and the ten acres to Suffolk County.

One fact that particularly interested Diane and I was that we were told "no lights stay on in the building when it's closed for the night." Diane asked questions about the lights a few times and in a few different ways to verify it was true. We didn't bother telling anyone we had been to the Manor several times late at night and had seen lights on in different rooms on the main floor.

However, the strangest thing that happened while we were taking the tour was that Diane's sunglasses were swiped off her head and tossed several feet through the air to the top of an old box piano. This happened while we were standing in a parlor built onto the house in 1772 by Isaac Gardiner and his wife Mary, both of whom are buried in the cemetery.

The glasses smacked down on top of the piano.

I had been looking at Diane at the second her sunglasses went flying off her head. I saw the glasses *lift off her head* and fly through the air as if by a magical power of their own. She immediately put her hand to the top of her head and looked around to see if anyone was near her, but, of course, nobody was there.

Startled, she asked, "Did you see that? Something just knocked the sunglasses off my head!"

She picked up her glasses from the piano, looked around, and said, "That was freaky!" Then she gave me a look that told me she had not been responsible for the occurrence, but I already knew that.

Was a spirit trying to communicate with Diane, perhaps encouraging her to play the old piano? Or was it a hostile spirit that wanted her out of the house? We'll probably never know.

A few of the docents we spoke with said they had been at a Halloween party in the mansion when they heard stomping and walking on the upper floor. When security investigated, there was nobody there. We were also told a "professional" photographer had photographed the cemetery, "and when the film was developed there were a lot of strange orbs and white clouds over the graves."

Ever See A Ghost?

A week after touring the house, Diane and I went back to the Manor and took a tour of the grounds with a guide. As the tour was winding down, we asked the guide, Celeste, if she had any paranormal experiences while in the mansion or on the property. We asked if she had ever seen a ghost.

While she said she had never seen a ghost, she did hear of people visiting the Manor who have reported unexplainable occurrences and some of whom said they saw apparitions.

When asked about slaves being buried on the property, the docent said there were no official records of slaves being buried there, but there was a strong likelihood slaves were buried in an unmarked area on the grounds.

Shall We Stay or Shall We Go?

In late March 2009, we invited John Altieri, a well-known psychic from North Babylon, to join us on a night investigation of the small family cemetery situated behind the mansion on the Manor's property.

Altieri turned off Montauk Highway and drove slowly up the rutted dirt road, past the elegant old house. He parked where we told him we'd meet him — toward the back of the property, not far from the old defunct stables. It was dark and he was alone. Apprehensively, he got out of his car and studied the shadowy landscape. Large trees loomed all around him. Suddenly, he was jolted by a strong mental image, as he told us, "I had a clear vision of an American Revolutionary War soldier hanged from a branch of the tree beside me."

The three of us grabbed our cameras and voice recorders and headed to the burial ground. The heavy iron gate groaned in protest as I pushed it slowly open. Brown leaves covering the ground crunched under our feet as we carefully walked among the dark graves. There were no flowers or knickknacks placed around the stones. Certainly, this was an old and forgotten place.

Altieri later said that as we were exploring and photographing the graveyard, "I felt as though someone was looking at us through the bars of the fence that surround the cemetery."

Altieri said that he also got a strong sense that slaves were buried somewhere in the woods in that area — that feeling was reaffirmed when weeks later he returned with us to the Manor and inspected the land located behind a potting shed in the courtyard. He said he had received "a very strong feeling" that eight to twelve slaves were buried in unmarked graves in that spot.

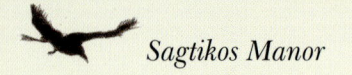

On this night, though, as the temperature dropped, the more creepier it became.

Suddenly I heard whispering and spotted two shadowy figures walking outside the cemetery fence. Excited it might be the ghosts of the Manor, I rushed out of the graveyard, leaving Diane and John behind. I shoved open the heavy iron gate and moved swiftly toward the voices. I pointed my camera in the direction of the whispers and quickly snapped off a shot.

The flash of my camera illuminated two images, but they were *not* spirits. The shadows turned out to be a pair of local ghost enthusiasts, a young man and woman. After introductions, I walked with the pair to the courtyard where the young man said he had photographed ghostly mists in the past.

While it was the young woman's first time at the Manor, the young man said he had been visiting there at night for a couple of years. Though he had several paranormal experiences on the property, his most dramatic experience occurred only two weeks ago while visiting the burial ground with two friends; one of whom refused to enter the graveyard.

"He felt very anxious about being there," the young man said of his friend.

Only two of them entered the cemetery, but they were not in there long when they, too, were overwhelmed by anxiety and felt like they were being told to leave. "I felt the spirits of the graveyard were telling us to get out," he said, so the two quickly left and all three friends fled the property.

Ironically, this experience would be duplicated by Diane and John on this very night.

Not long after the young ghost hunters left, I rejoined Diane and John in the graveyard. I was getting ready to tell them the story of the young man's experience of being driven out of the cemetery when, suddenly and without a word Diane bolted past me and out through the iron gate!

"I got the overwhelming sense I needed to leave the graveyard," she later reported. "I shoved open the gate and ran. When I reached my car, I took several long, deep breaths until a sense of calm returned. I was filled with dread, but I didn't know why!"

Diane turned to find John Altieri coming toward her. He was walking quickly and his face was white. Diane noted: "You look like you've just seen a ghost."

"I was being told to leave the graveyard." Altieri answered. "I kept hearing it was time to leave. Leave! Leave!"

"That's why I left, too!" Diane exclaimed. "I didn't hear or see anything, but I knew I had to leave."

They both looked back toward the mysterious graveyard where I was alone — *or was I?*

On this spirit-filled night, Diane places her voice recorder on a sarcophagus in the Gardiner-Thompson Cemetery at Sagtikos Manor.

8

Mount Olivet & All Faiths Cemeteries

Middle Village / Maspeth

Locations: *Mount Olivet Cemetery* is on Grand Avenue in Maspeth, Queens. *All Faiths Cemetery* is on Metropolitan Avenue in Middle Village, Queens,

Description: These large neighboring cemeteries are separated by Eliot Avenue.

Mount Olivet Cemetery: Take the Long Island Expressway west to exit #19 (69th Street and Grand Avenue). Go to the second traffic light and turn left on Grand Avenue. Cemetery entrance is approximately 1/4 of a mile on the left.

All Faiths Cemetery: Take the Long Island Expressway to Exit 19 and follow to the Grand Avenue/69th Street Exit. Follow Service Road of LIE to 69th Street and make a left heading south. Take 69th Street south for about 2.0 miles and make a right on Metropolitan Avenue. Go to the second gate to enter. The Cemetery Administration Office will be on the right.

Mount Olivet Cemetery, Maspeth, Queens

Mount Olivet & All Faiths Cemeteries

A ghost moves through Mount Olivet Cemetery. *Drawing by Karen Isaksen.*

Wandering Ghosts

Neighboring Queens cemeteries, Mount Olivet and All Faiths (formerly known as Lutheran), have no affiliation with each other — *except maybe for some wandering ghosts*.

A narrow road, which today is Eliot Avenue, separates the two haunted properties. This same road has been used by ghosts as they wander between the enormous graveyards, pursued by people who could hear the spirits moaning, and in some cases, even see them.

In 1936, a photographer caught the image of a ghost crossing the road from Mount Olivet Cemetery to Lutheran Cemetery, and other evidence supporting the existence of ghosts at these cemeteries is substantial. Some ghost sightings have been documented in newspapers while others have been reported by visitors and cemetery workers.

The Dead Unburied

Should the dead be unburied?

For thousands of dearly departed Manhattan residents there was no choice. Two cholera epidemics, occurring seventeen years apart, caused over 7,000 deaths in Manhattan. The government feared that the decomposing bodies of cholera victims would contaminate the island's precious well water. Thus, a law was passed in 1852 halting all burials in Manhattan.

Through the early 1900s the decomposing and skeletal remains of many thousands of New York City residents were transported in the dead of night from Manhattan to newly established cemeteries across the East River in Queens.

Mount Olivet Cemetery, Maspeth, and Lutheran Cemetery, now All Faiths, in Middle Village, were among the final destinations for many of the corpses — and it is in these two cemeteries located next to each other that neighborhood residents, cemetery employees, and visitors have *heard* and *seen* ghosts. Are these the ghosts of people who were unburied and moved?

All Faiths Cemetery, formerly Lutheran Cemetery, Middle Village, Queens.

Chasing Ghosts in Queens

In the summer of 1884, neighbors told Town Constable Henry Bosch of Fresh Pond that they saw a "spook" and described the ghost as "a tall man, well-built, and perfectly nude."

One late afternoon several women picking peas on a farm bordering Mount Olivet Cemetery heard groans of distress

Mount Olivet & All Faiths Cemeteries

This orb (circled) shot out of the ground at night in **All Faiths Cemetery**. Though there are no gravestones in this area, bodies are still interred in this ground. Gravestones are optional at **All Faiths Cemetery**.

coming from the graveyard. The *New York Times* reported on July 27, 1884 that the women "went toward the voice, which they followed to the edge of a pool, where it faded away to a hollow groan."

The frightened women ran to the home of their employer, the farmer, Mr. Ring, and reported what they had heard. No amount of pleading or cajoling could force the women back into the fields, so Mr. Ring took the terrified women to see Constable Bosch where they repeated their story. Bosch gathered a posse of ten men and headed out to the cemetery to investigate the strange sounds.

It was twilight when Bosch's posse reached the gates of Mount Olivet Cemetery. A man in the group stated he wasn't going into the graveyard at night and announced he was going home. The other nine members of the posse also decided on the spot it was best that they return home as well.

When Constable Bosch and his timid posse arrived back at Bosch's house, they found neighborhood residents gathered there. According to the *New York Times*, one of the women in the crowd stated emphatically that she, too, had seen the ghost. The woman described the apparition as "tall and thin, always dressed in white." She added the ghost was brandishing "a large carving knife."

The July 27, 1884 edition of the *Brooklyn Eagle* reported that another woman in the crowd that evening also claimed to have seen the same ghost, but Mrs. Nellie McCormick claimed the knife-carrying ghost the two women saw was that of her dead fiancé, Mike Kelly. She stated he had committed suicide after she jilted him and married Mr. Tim McCormick. She claimed Mike Kelly's ghost followed her to America from Ireland. Now, no matter where she and her husband move, Mike Kelly's ghost is sure to follow.

A gravedigger and a stonecutter, both highly regarded men in the community, reported to Constable Bosch that they also had heard mysterious cries while working in Mount Olivet Cemetery.

Newspaper reports stated that Constable Bosch gathered fifty men, all armed with shotguns, to search Mount Olivet Cemetery. The following report was printed in the *Brooklyn Eagle*:

"There they heard the mysterious voice, and the whole party advanced toward it, but try as hard as they could, it always kept the same distance from them. They went tramping through the mud for almost a mile, until they reached Lutheran Cemetery where the mysterious voice ceased and could be made to speak no more."

The entire community was frightened when no source for the sounds could be found.

Resident Ghosts of All Faiths

While we were on a late night tour at All Faiths Cemetery, Brian Chavanne, the assistant director of operations, pointed out an area that was once a large pond. In later years the pond was filled in to accommodate more gravesites, he said.

"People see Indians where the pond used to be," said Chavanne, "then the Indians take off into the trees and vanish."

While maintaining a skeptical stance of the paranormal, Chavanne acknowledged that odd and unexplainable events do occur in the graveyard. Chavanne, though, a twenty-two year employee of the cemetery, terms the events "abnormal" ... *not* paranormal:

Mount Olivet & All Faiths Cemeteries

The original plaque for the Lutheran Cemetery now known as All Faiths Cemetery in Middle Village, Queens.

Mount Olivet & All Faiths Cemeteries

Site of former pond at All Faiths Cemetery where apparitions of Native American Indians have been seen. Cemetery personnel report the Indians typically run off into the trees.

One night he said he saw a purple mist floating amid the graves. He rationalized the event by saying he believes the purple mist was a result of escaping gases from embalmed corpses buried in the ground. Specifically, he said he believes this was a chemical reaction caused by formaldehyde, a preservative used in the embalming process.

He also reported that while patrolling the cemetery at night he's heard human whistling that lasts longer than any human could whistle. The whistling typically occurs during the Halloween season. He attributes the sound to wind blowing through the trees, but concedes the trees are usually bare by the end of October.

A variety of other "abnormal" events have occurred at the cemetery over the years for which Chavanne said he has no explanation. These include finding doors he had locked unlocked, lights he had turned off, on; and he said he's seen shadowy figures, but does not believe the shadows were ghosts.

Nearing midnight during the tour we stopped by the cemetery's main office building. In the dark, Chavanne was searching his keychain for the key to the office door when suddenly a spotlight in front of the building flared on.

We asked if the spotlight was on a timer or motion activated, but Chavanne shook his head. As we stood there the light went out, plunging us back into darkness. Several seconds later, it illuminated again. Chavanne said an engineer had checked the spotlight and said he could find no fault with the circuit. He has no explanation for the malfunction. We suggested that it might well be a playful cemetery ghost.

Death Takes a Holiday

It was 4:30 a.m. June 15, 1904. Magdalena Herzog awoke gasping from the recurring nightmare.

"Lena, Lena! Everything is fine! You're safe, I'm right here!" said her startled husband Ernst. He wrapped his powerful suntanned arms around her. Her white nightgown stuck to her sweaty body.

"Was it the same dream?" Ernst asked.

"It was horrible," Lena cried. "One minute I'm in the sunshine playing with Helga, and the next we are surrounded in blackness. Then we're being pulled down!" She began crying anew. "I can't catch my breath, and I can't find the baby!"

"It's only a bad dream," said Ernst. He kissed her wet cheek.

"It felt real!" she whispered.

The honey dawn light trickled across the patched quilt and onto the bare wood floor of the tiny colorless bedroom they

Mount Olivet & All Faiths Cemeteries

Engraving of the *General Slocum* burning in the East River. Reprint licensed through The Mariners' Museum, Newport News, Virginia.

shared with their baby daughter, Helga. It was their first home in America; a two-room flat on the third floor of a dingy brick building. The cold water walk-up was in Germantown, Lower East Side, Manhattan.

Lena jumped out of bed and flew to the crib to check on baby Helga. Ernst tiptoed up behind his wife and peeked over her shoulder. "Like an angel!" he whispered.

Lena took a deep shuddering breath and put her finger to her lips. She took her husband's hand and led him to the kitchen. She was still trembling from the dream.

Ernst wanted to take Lena's mind off the nightmare, so he asked, "Do you have everything ready for the boat ride today?"

"Everything is ready, but maybe we should stay home."

"Stay home!" Ernst's voice rose angrily. "We had to save for months so you and Helga could go on this boat trip. Are we that rich that you can just throw my money away?"

Lena looked down at the floor. "No, Ernst, of course not."

Ernst saw the stricken look on his wife's face. He put out his arms. "Come here, my love."

Lena walked over. He held her close. She rested her head on his broad shoulder and inhaled the comforting scent of his skin.

Lena had hardly been out of the apartment since Helga was born. Ernst thought this trip would give her the chance to mingle with the other neighborhood women. He cupped her chin in his large calloused hand and looked into her crystal blue eyes. She looked scared.

"Once you're aboard the *General Slocum* and heading out of the city, you'll feel better," he reassured her. "We've never been to Long Island. Promise me you'll remember every detail and tell me all about it. Besides think of all the fun you'll have with the other ladies, gossiping and telling stories about the old country. I know how much you ladies love to gossip!"

Lena's mouth curved into a smile that didn't quite reach her eyes.

"I saw your blue hat with the big red feather on the dresser. I don't think you should wear it today."

"Why not, Ernst?" Lena asked.

"The other ladies will be jealous of such an elegant hat!" he boomed.

This time the smile reached her eyes.

Suddenly the baby began crying. "Let me get her," said Ernst.

Lena watched as her husband disappeared into the bedroom.

All her friends told her what a lucky woman she was. Most husbands ignored their children, but not her Ernst. Helga was the light of his life. He held her, fed her, and even changed her. Lena's friends couldn't believe any man would do that!

Ernst came back cuddling his blond, blue-eyed daughter. "Here is our beautiful girl, Mama! Wide awake and ready for today's big adventure!"

"Give me the baby and eat your breakfast, Ernst," said Lena.

He planted a kiss on Helga's blond curls, and handed the baby over to his wife.

Fire Aboard General Slocum!

Hell Gate is the narrow channel of the East River swirling its way into the Long Island Sound. It was in this body of treacherous water in 1904 that the worst maritime disaster in New York State history took place — the *General Slocum* disaster.

It was June 15th, a sunny mild day — the perfect weather for a picnic. Members of St. Mark's Lutheran Church in Germantown, Lower Manhattan, boarded the *General Slocum*, a newly renovated steamboat, for an excursion to a beach on Long Island.

Mount Olivet & All Faiths Cemeteries

Survivors of the *General Slocum* disaster on North Brother Island. *From the Maggie Land Blanck Collection, Harper's Weekly, June 25, 1904*

The Third Street pier was crowded with cheerful onlookers waving to the lucky people, mostly women and children dressed in their Sunday best, who were leaving the steamy city for a day of fun.

A Trip to Paradise

Lena reluctantly followed some of the neighborhood women up the gangplank of the enormous steamer. Her feelings of foreboding increased with each step and she clasped Helga tightly to her breast to keep her safe.

"Let's hurry so we can get seats on the top," said Mrs. Schmidt. "My mister told me it's the best spot on the whole boat!"

Lena's instincts told her she and Helga should get off the boat now, but she feared Ernst would be furious with her. When the women reached the top deck, Lena politely excused herself. She needed to escape. Her panic was reaching a crescendo. Scenes of the nightmare flashed in her head. She was terrified.

The cacophony of music and singing, boat whistles and horns, cheering and screaming, and the thuds of the pounding engine overwhelmed poor baby Helga. She began crying. Lena found an empty place by the rail and rocked the baby. She pressed her lips close to Helga's ear and crooned a soothing lullaby.

With flags flying, the band on board playing a lively tune, and all three decks crowded with happy passengers, the paddle wheeler glided from the dock and headed up the East River to "Hell Gate." Meanwhile, somewhere

Route on the East River that the *General Slocum* took on the day it caught fire. *From the Maggie Land Blanck Collection.*

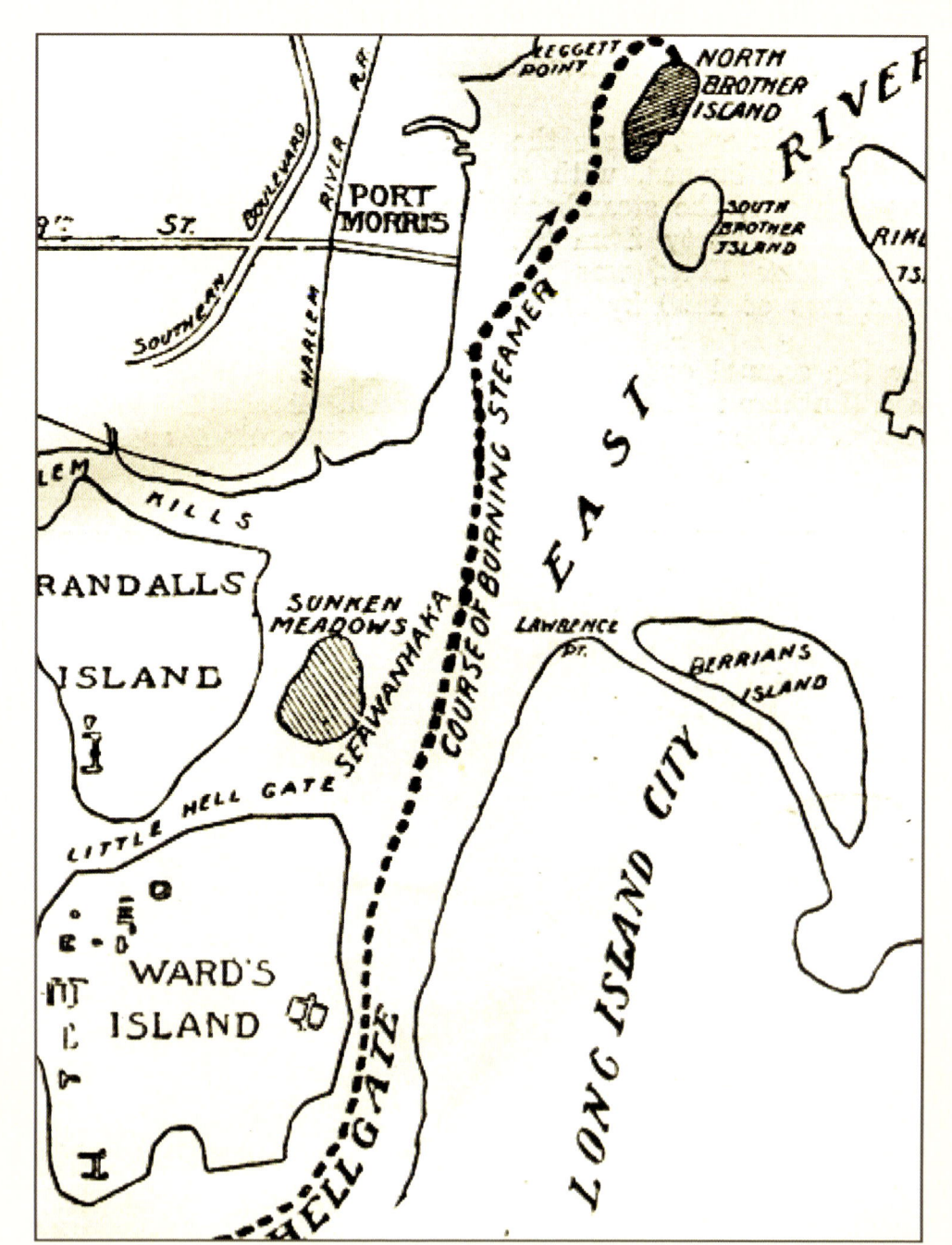

Mount Olivet & All Faiths Cemeteries

below deck, an ember, possibly from a match or a cigarette, was about to ignite canisters of kerosene, gallons of oil paint, dry hay, and wooden barrels.

Thick black smoke billowed and flames from below deck quickly engulfed the fast moving vessel just as the *Slocum* entered Hell Gate, where the Triborough Bridge stands today.

The *New York Times* reported, "All this time full speed ahead was maintained, and the flames fanned fiercely by the wind ate their way swiftly toward the hapless women and babies that were crowded on all the decks astern."

Ernst navigated his clumsy horse-drawn ice wagon down brown cobblestone streets crowded with shouting fishmongers and rickety wooden vegetable stands. The hot June air was thick and stagnant with the mixture of odors from the fish and rotting vegetables. Sweat stained Ernst's dark blue work shirt at the collar and under his arms.

The *General Slocum* steamship. *From the Maggie Land Blanck Collection.*

Children darted in and out of the street, running behind his creaky wagon, daring each other to steal a piece of precious ice on this hot summer morning. Ernst halted his wagon and half-heartedly scolded the children who scurried off and disappeared into the crowds.

Approaching the Third Street pier, Ernst was surprised to see the *General Slocum* still tied to the dock. It was supposed to depart at 8:45 and now it was nearly 9:30. Was something wrong? He jumped from the wagon and rushed into the local tavern.

"Patrick, why is the *Slocum* still docked?" he asked the bartender. "Is there something wrong with her?"

"Ah...no doubt tis the good pastor that's responsible," Patrick Feeney answered with his thick Irish brogue. "The man's got a soft heart. He delayed the ship so the stragglers wouldn't be left behind."

Ernst dashed out to the pier and pushed his way through the throngs of people. He shielded his eyes from the sun and scanned the three decks. Good God, there were so many passengers! It would take a miracle for him to catch a glimpse of Lena and Helga!

Then he saw the tall red feather sticking out of Lena's blue hat. Lena loved that feathered hat. It was the finest thing she owned. She acted elegant in it. Ernst always hated that hat, especially the feather, but now the gaudy red feather was waving in the gentle breeze like a beacon.

Ernst shouted and waved. It was impossible for Lena to hear him above the noise of the crowd. Relatives and friends of the passengers aboard the *Slocum* were cheering and singing madly. For Ernst, the din receded into the background as he watched his wife cradling their baby in her arms, rocking Helga back and forth. He could almost hear Lena's sweet voice crooning Braham's Lullaby. Even in that silly blue hat with the red feather, Lena looked beautiful — just like an angel.

Black Saturday – The Burials

Most of the 1,021 dead from the *General Slocum* disaster were buried in Lutheran Cemetery in Middle Village, Queens.

The first twenty-nine unidentified victims, who were burned beyond recognition, were buried side-by-side in a long trench. Thousands of people attended the mass funeral. Many other mourners in black were already in the cemetery burying their own dead from the *Slocum* as the mass funeral got underway.

Victims of the *General Slocum* disaster. From the Maggie Land Blanck Collection, the New York Times, June 16, 1904.

Mount Olivet & All Faiths Cemeteries

Angel and Child

The bodies of Magdalena and Helga Herzog were never recovered. Ernst stayed in the tiny walk-up he once shared with his wife and daughter. He kept Lena's blue hat with the red feather on the dresser in their bedroom. It was the only trace of his wife the morgue could provide. That silly blue hat became his most treasured possession.

Ernst visited Lutheran Cemetery every week without fail until his death in 1940.

In 1912, two towering statues were dedicated at the Slocum Memorial: one was an angel blowing a trumpet; the other, an angel holding a child. Ernst would stand below the statue with the child and stare, as he often thought, "Helga's hair would be long like that now."

If he was still enough, he could hear Lena's lilting voice singing the familiar Braham's Lullaby as Helga giggled and cooed in her arms. Sometimes he swore he saw the angel swaying as though she was rocking the child. It reminded him of the last time he had seen his wife and daughter on the upper deck of the *General Slocum*.

The *General Slocum* Memorial at All Faiths Cemetery.

Photo of the *General Slocum* sinking off North Brother Island after the fire. Of the 1,358 people aboard that day, 1,021 perished, mostly women and children. It was the worst disaster in New York City's history up until terrorists destroyed the Twin Towers at the World Trade Center on September 11, 2001. *From the Maggie Land Blanck Collection, Harper's Weekly, June 25, 1904.*

View of riverfront showing bodies cast up on shore. *From the Maggie Land Blanck Collection, Harper's Weekly, June 25, 1904.*

The dead were laid out on the beach at North Brother Island. *From the Maggie Land Blanck Collection, Harper's Weekly, June 25, 1904.*

A Mother's Premonition

Lena fought the panic that was rising inside her as the *General Slocum* moved away from the dock. The big paddle wheel churned up the water with loud slaps and splashes, but the steamer glided smoothly up the East River and Lena soon felt more at ease. The view from the upper deck was something she had never seen before. She wished Ernst was here to see it with her.

Helga stirred in Lena's arms. "Are you having fun, my sweet baby?"

Helga giggled as her mother tickled her under her chin.

Lena took a deep, relaxing breath. She thought she smelled something burning. She heard one of the other passengers say that the smoke was coming from the galley. She continued to play with the baby.

Suddenly, the acrid smell of burning kerosene and paint choked the fresh sea air. Black smoke rose from the lower decks and soon obliterated the blue sky. People began screaming and stampeded toward the back of the steamer to escape the flames and smoke. Lena clutched her baby daughter and pulled the blanket over her face. "Oh God, please help me!" she prayed, as she tried to keep from being trampled.

Lena could not escape the heat and smoke. She felt rumbling and shaking beneath her feet. There was a deafening explosion and the baby was torn from her arms.

Lena was swallowed by a gaping hole that opened in the floor. She slammed into the hardwood of the main deck and was thrown into the black water of the East River. Her last thought was of her baby as the water closed over her.

A Tragic End

The *Slocum's* skipper, Captain Van Schaick, later stated that he looked out from the pilothouse and saw "a fierce blaze — the wildest I have ever seen."

"I started to head for 134th Street, but was warned off by the captain of a tugboat who shouted to me that the boat would set fire to the lumber yards and oil tanks there. Besides, I knew that the shore was lined with rocks and the boat would founder if I put it there. I then fixed upon North Brother Island."

"I stuck to my post in the pilothouse until my cap caught fire. We were then about 25 feet off North Brother Island. She went on the beach; bow on, in about 25 feet of water. Most of the people aft, where the fire raged fiercest, jumped in when we were in deep water and were carried away. We had no chance to lower the lifeboats. They were burned before the crew could get at them."

The City Health Commissioner was inspecting the hospital on North Brother Island that day. He later stated, "I will never be able to forget the scene...the utter horror of it. Along the beach the boats were carrying in the living and the dying and towing in the dead."

Of the 1,358 who boarded the ship that morning, 1,021 perished. On January 26, 2004, the last survivor of the *General Slocum* tragedy, the deadliest disaster in New York City history until September 11, 2001, died at age 100. Her name was Adella Wotherspoon and as the *New York Times* aptly pointed out, "She was the youngest *Slocum* survivor having at last become the oldest."

Opposite: North Brother Island as it appears today from the end of East 149th Street in the Bronx. The island is where the doomed *General Slocum* wrecked when it was burning. It is currently uninhabited, but at the time of the disaster, it housed a hospital for people with contagious diseases.

The Midnight Hour

During a late night tour of All Faiths Cemetery, sounds carried from miles across the rolling hills: Diane heard a child whimpering and felt the sudden rush of a ghostly wind fly by her in the still night air as she stood in front of the Slocum Memorial while Joe heard far away screaming as he was photographing the same area.

Flanking the main memorial are the statues of two angels: one with a trumpet; the other holding a child. The angel holding the child is pointing downward. We asked Chavanne if he knew why the angel was pointing down. He said he al-

All Faiths Assistant Director of Operations, Brian Chavanne, and Diane Hill listen to the eerie sounds of the night at the Memorial for sixty-one unidentified victims of the *General Slocum* Disaster of 1904.

Mount Olivet & All Faiths Cemeteries

Mount Olivet & All Faiths Cemeteries

ways thought the angel was pointing out the children who needed to be brought to heaven.

We asked Chavanne what the angel with the trumpet symbolized, but he didn't know. We decided the angel with the trumpet was the messenger, calling other angels for help with the children.

Today is June 15th, the anniversary of the *General Slocum* disaster. A gentle breeze caresses the trees as we stand before the memorial in All Faiths Cemetery. The grass is green and vibrant summer flowers decorate the site. High white clouds float lazily across the blue summer sky.

The contrast between life and death is profound, but for today, at least, the haunting spirits of the graveyard seem to be at rest. Tomorrow, though, is another day.

(Author's Note: We give a special thanks to Daniel Austin, Jr., president of the All Faiths Restoration and Beautification Program for striving to preserve the past for future generations. To donate a tax deductible contribution to the All Faiths Cemetery restoration effort, contact Mr. Austin at 718-821-1750.)

Opposite: Security personnel at All Faiths Cemetery reported hearing screams from the area of the *General Slocum* Memorial. There are sixty-one unidentified victims from the Slocum tragedy buried at this site. Hundreds of other victims of the boat fire are buried throughout the graveyard. Several of the night security staff reported seeing the angel statue at the Slocum Memorial *rocking* the baby in her arms.

The General Slocum Memorial at All Faiths Cemetery.

Bibliography

"A Haunted Woman." *Brooklyn Eagle*, July 27, 1884.

"A Monosyllabic Ghost." *Brooklyn Eagle*, July 28, 1884.

Amon, Rhona. "The Cemetery Belt." *Newsday*. (Retrieved from Juniper Park Civic Association's website www.junipercivic.com.)

"Following an Elusive Voice." *New York Times*, July 27, 1884.

Hammond, John E. *Historic Cemeteries of Oyster Bay: A Guide to Their Locations and Sources of Transcription Information*. Oyster Bay, New York: Town of Oyster Bay Historian's Office, 2007.

"History of Sagtikos Manor." Sagtikos Manor Historical Society *(www.sagtikosmanor.com/history.html)*.

Homan, Beecher. "The Suffolk County Alms-House." *Yaphank As It Is and Was*. Self-published, 1875. *(www.longwood.k12.ny.us/history/yaphank/almshouse.html)*

Juniper Park Civic Association *(www.junipercivic.com)*

Long Island Oddities *(www.lioddities.com/ghost/unioncem.html)*

"National Register Information System." National Register of Historic Places. National Park Service, January 23, 2007 *(www.nr.nps.gov)*.

O'Donnell, Edward T. *Ship Ablaze*. New York, New York: Broadway Books, 2003.

Office of Suffolk County Clerk: Historical Documents. "Suffolk County Almshouse of Suffolk County: A Finding Aid to the Records 1871–1953." *(www.wotan.liu.edu/~mptakacs/pottersfieldimage.html)*

"The End to a Journey's End (circa 1936-1938)." WPA Project 1185. *(www.wotan.liu.edu/~mptakacs/almshouserecords.html)*

Warren, Ed and Lorraine, and Robert David Chase. *Graveyard*. New York, New York: St. Martin's Paperbacks, 1992.

Index

Adams, Tennessee, 120
All Faiths Cemetery, 123, 125-129, 136, 141, 143

Baldwin, 26
Bay Shore, 78, 111
Bohemia, 21
Brookhaven, 5

East Hampton, 7, 9
East Hillside Cemetery, 54-56, 60, 62, 65, 66, 71, 72
Easton, Connecticut, 89, 91, 92, 96

Farmingdale, 105
Farmingville, 4
Freeport, 38
Fresh Pond, 125

Germantown, 131
Glen Head, 54

Hampton Bays, 6, 9, 10, 29, 53
Hempstead, 46, 47, 50, 51, 53
Hempstead Plains, 51
Hoosac Train Tunnel, 78

Lake Ronkonkoma, 9, 17, 19, 21, 74-78, 100
Lutheran Cemetery, 125, 127, 128, 135, 136

Machpelah Cemetery, 63, 65
Manhattan, 10, 125, 131
Maspeth, 123, 125
Massachusetts, 39, 41, 78
Massapequa Park, 102
Melville, 18, 65
Middle Island, 80, 82 85, 89, 92

Middle Village, 123, 125, 128, 135
Mount Olivet Cemetery, 123-125, 127

New York, 18, 21, 35, 37, 125, 131, 137, 141
North Adams, Massachusetts, 39, 78
North Babylon, 105, 121

Oyster Bay, 97, 99, 119

Patchogue, 120
Pine Hollow Cemetery, 97-100, 102-106, 108
Potters Field, 6, 11, 13-45, 100

Queens, 29, 65, 123, 125, 128, 135

Ridgewood, 63, 65
Rocky Point, 92
Ronkonkoma, 26

Sag Harbor, 7-9
Sagtikos Manor, 109-112, 115, 118, 119
Southampton, 7, 8, 29, 82
St. George's Cemetery, 46, 47, 49, 51, 53
St. George's Episcopal Church, 46, 47
Sweet Hollow Road, 18, 41, 65, 85, 106

Tennessee, 120

Union Cemetery, 80-89, 91-93, 95, 96

West Bay Shore, 109, 111
West Hempstead, 51
West Sayville, 29

Yaphank, 6, 11, 15-17, 30, 31, 35, 37, 100